Deadlier than the Male

Deadlier than the Male

Wives of the Generals 1677–1937

Trina Beckett

Pen & Sword
MILITARY

First published in Great Britain in 2018 by
PEN & SWORD MILITARY
An imprint of
Pen & Sword Books Ltd
Yorkshire – Philadelphia

ISBN 9781781590133

Typeset in Ehrhardt MT by SRJ Info Jnana System Pvt Ltd.

Printed and bound by TJ International Ltd, Padstow, Cornwall

Pen & Sword Books Ltd incorporates the Imprints of Aviation, Atlas, Family
History, Fiction, Maritime, Military, Discovery, Politics, History, Archaeology,
Select, Wharncliffe Local History, Wharncliffe True Crime, Military Classics,
Wharncliffe Transport, Leo Cooper, The Praetorian Press, Remember When,
White Owl, Seaforth Publishing and Frontline Publishing.

For a complete list of Pen & Sword titles please contact
PEN & SWORD BOOKS LTD
47 Church Street, Barnsley, South Yorkshire, S70 2AS, England
E-mail: enquiries@pen-and-sword.co.uk
Website: www.pen-and-sword.co.uk

Or

PEN & SWORD BOOKS
1950 Lawrence Rd, Havertown, PA 19083, USA
E-mail: Uspen-and-sword@casematepublishers.com
Website: www.penandswordbooks.com

Contents

List of Illustrations

Sarah, Duchess of Marlborough.
John, Duke of Marlborough.
Catherine 'Kitty', Duchess of Wellington.
Arthur Wellesley, Duke of Wellington.
Juana, Lady Smith
Louisa, Lady Wolseley.
Sir Robert Sale.
Nora, Lady Roberts.
Florentia, Lady Sale.
Dorothy, Lady Haig.
Sir Douglas Haig.
Bernard Montgomery with his son David, 1943.

Acknowledgments

Quotations from the Royal Archives appear by gracious permission of Her Majesty the Queen. I also wish to acknowledge my thanks to the following for their courtesy and kind permission in allowing me to consult and quote from archives in their possession and/or copyright: Sir Richard Pole-Carew Bt., and the Marquis of Salisbury. Similarly, thanks for allowing consultation and/or quotation from archives in their possession and/or copyright is due to the courtesy and kind permission of the Trustees of the British Library; Cornwall County Record Office; Devon County Record Office; the David M. Rubenstein Rare Books and Manuscript Library of Duke University; the Campbell Collections (formerly the Killie Campbell Africana Library) of the University of KwaZulu-Natal; the KwaZulu-Natal Archives; the Trustees of the Liddell Hart Centre for Military Archives, King's College, London; the National Army Museum; the National Library of Ireland; the National Library of Scotland; the National Library of Wales; the National War Museum, Edinburgh; Queen Mary University Library; the Royal Pavilion Libraries and Museum (Hove Public Library); South Lanarkshire Council Museum; and Warwickshire County Record Office.

***

Filling at least the top five places of my 'grateful thanks' list is my husband Ian. He has supported me in every area of my life, and this has been no exception. You can't be married to a published military historian without an interest in the subject rubbing off! I felt that Ian had dealt with the men, so thought I would see what some of the wives had been up to. He discovered for me more books on my subjects than I could ever have imagined, which is one of the reasons my research took so long; that plus a gap of one year due to eye surgery.

My daughter Andrea (a published medieval historian) helped me with style, and my son Mark (my IT guru) unpicked some tricky formatting problems. My whole family have spurred me on when, at times, I came close to giving up.

I have been inspired by my grandchildren Naomi, Abigail and Jackson, whose writing achievements at school proved the impetus for me to resurrect a dusty dream. Hard to know what Alex, just three, makes of it all, but he does love being read to!

A mention also for my friend Maureen, who has shown such a positive interest in this book since its embryonic stage that I simply had to get on with it.

Thanks must go to Rupert Harding and the team at Pen and Sword, who actually remembered who I am, blew the cobwebs off my contract and went ahead with publication.

Finally, my grateful thanks to Morrab Library, a private subscription library in Penzance with no computers in sight, but whose staff clambered up ladders to find old tomes that hadn't seen the light of day for many years.

TMB,
January 2018.

Introduction

British military wives have tended to be studied, if at all, in terms of the ordinary rank and file soldiers, especially in popular literature.[1] Academic studies have concentrated almost exclusively on the wives of ordinary soldiers.[2]

By contrast there has been far less interest in officers' wives. Historians have tended to dismiss the army wife as an 'incorporated wife', subordinated to her husband's institution and, therefore, something of a victim in playing a predetermined subservient role. Additionally, feminist historians have seen such a woman's status as deriving entirely from that of her husband, with any potential influence over the husband's career represented in negative terms. While it is recognized that women might enjoy considerable authority in the private domestic sphere, there has been an assumption that even women with apparent influence in the public sphere, such as the great political hostesses, lacked genuine power.[3]

The old military adage applied to officers was that 'subalterns must not marry, captains may marry, majors should marry and colonels must marry'. However, through the nineteenth century, increasing numbers of officers were married men. The proportion of officers who were married rose from 25.4 per cent in 1851 to 33.5 per cent in 1871, although the proportion of married officers under the age of 25 remained small.[4]

The wives of ordinary officers had a similar role in relation to the wives of other ranks as their husbands did to their men; the same went for the wives of senior officers in relation to those of junior officers.[5] It has been said that the higher an officer progressed through the ranks, the higher the intonation of the voice of the wife! In the case of senior soldiers, the military wife has been largely 'hidden from history'. In the 600 pages of the two volumes of Field Marshal Sir Evelyn Wood's autobiography, *From*

Midshipman to Field Marshal, he mentions Lady Wood on only eleven pages. Two of these references concern her marriage and two her death.[6] Yet, as will be shown, Lady Wood played a not-inconsiderable part in her husband's career.

When a wife *is* mentioned, it is often less than illuminating, as in the sixty-seven references to Lady Roberts in the 601 pages of the single-volume edition of Field Marshal Lord Roberts's *Forty One Years in India*, all of which simply mention her in passing as being present on this or that occasion.[7]

Where officers' wives have been a greater focus, the emphasis has been upon what might be termed their social role, as in a study of wives of officers serving in British India in the first half of the nineteenth century comparing them with those of officers serving on the American frontier.[8] Very few studies of leading soldiers' wives attempt to assess their influence, one such being Celia Lee's biography of Jean, Lady Hamilton. There is also an essay collection on the wives of some prominent Union and Confederate generals in the American Civil War.[9]

Since the wife's public status was most likely to derive from that of her husband, it is likely that many wives would wish to protect and enhance their husbands' careers. In doing so, they may go well beyond what might be termed mere duty, and wield effective power or influence over their husbands' careers. This seems an obvious point to make, but it is one that many historians who have studied the 'incorporated wife' appear too ready to dismiss. One study, touching on the preparation of Victorian girls for marriage through finishing schools, argues that 'the optimism of many generations of young middle-class English girls has been sustained by a belief in the myth that behind every successful man is a good woman'.[10]

It seems appropriate, therefore, to attempt to assess the degree to which officers' wives influenced military careers, whether or not they observed the existence of 'separate spheres' and whether or not their 'incorporation' truly implied their 'subordination' within the army. What follows is a study of a number of the wives of leading British soldiers from the late seventeenth to the twentieth centuries. It begins with Sarah Churchill, Duchess of Marlborough, whose role as a confidante of Queen Anne was central to Marlborough's survival as commander-in-chief of the army in Flanders during the War of the Spanish Succession. By contrast, Catherine 'Kitty' Pakenham's family's initial rejection of the future Duke of Wellington's proposed marriage to their daughter played a pivotal role in setting him upon his military career.

Juana, Lady Smith and Florentia, Lady Sale were both indomitable women and courageous in the extreme. Juana in particular proved far more popular than Sir Harry Smith in his posts in India and South Africa, while Florentia became a far more noted celebrity than Sir Robert Sale. Wives of later Victorian generals such as Louisa, Viscountess Wolseley, Paulina, Lady Wood, Edith, Lady Colley and Nora, Countess Roberts offer fascinating and divergent case studies of influence attempted and influence achieved. Dorothy, Countess Haig emerges from the shadow of Douglas Haig as a figure just as complex as her husband. As an epilogue, Betty Montgomery adds to her astonishing influence as a spouse an extension beyond the grave of the significance of a deceased wife in the fashioning of the character of Bernard Montgomery.

The wives of leading soldiers did play a significant role behind the scenes. In so doing, they were not necessarily confined by any perception of separate private and public spheres. The incorporation of women in the army through marriage neither automatically implied their subordination nor constrained their ambition. As Frank Prochaska has remarked, 'We are perhaps too prone to see limitations where the women of the past saw possibilities'.[11]

COVER. COVER.—"So glad to see you, Mrs. Bamsby! And how is your dear husband? Where *is* the Colonel? I was only saying the other day, 'I wonder when I shall see Colonel Bamsby!'" *Mrs. Colonel B.* "You'll see him *now*, my dear, if I just step aside, or you walk round me."

Cartoon from Punch.

Chapter 1

Petticoat Power: Sarah Churchill

At midnight on 25 November 1688, during the Glorious Revolution, two women slipped down a back staircase that linked two apartments in Whitehall. Still in their nightclothes, one lost her shoe in the mud of Pall Mall. They met a clergyman, hiding nearby to await them. Spirited in a coach from Charing Cross to the clergyman's house in Aldersgate Street, the party fled to Epping at daybreak. At the King's orders, guards arrived at the front of their apartments at 3.00 am but had been instructed not to disturb the inhabitants. Consequently the flight, which threw the authorities into near hysteria, was not discovered until the women were already well on their way to safety in Nottingham.

The escape was later portrayed as one woman unnecessarily frightening the other into deserting her own father, but the danger was real enough for those involved. The clergyman was Henry Compton, Bishop of London. The women's husbands were Prince George of Denmark and Lieutenant General Lord Churchill, who had both slipped away from the King's army during the previous two days. The woman who lost her shoe was Princess Anne, daughter of King James II, and her close confidante, accused of engineering the escape, Sarah Churchill.

The episode cemented the already close relationship between the 28-year-old Sarah and the 23-year-old Princess, who had known each other since Sarah had entered the service of James's first wife as a maid of honour in 1673. At this stage, John Churchill's influence with the Princess was of a more subordinate nature than that of his wife, but his career was beginning to reap the benefits of her close association. His contribution to the Revolution was rewarded with an earldom. An extinct peerage on his mother's side provided the title of Marlborough. Some sneered at

Marlborough, as a 'general of favour'.[1] But Marlborough, elevated to a dukedom upon Anne's accession in 1702, proved to be one of the greatest of all British generals. His stunning series of victories over the French during the War of the Spanish Succession at Blenheim (13 August 1704), Ramillies (23 May 1706), Oudenarde (11 July 1708), and Malplaquet (11 September 1709) testified to his military genius.

However, Sarah's influence over Anne not only sustained Marlborough's career amidst a controversial war, but also prolonged the administration of Marlborough's close political ally, Sidney Godolphin. Godolphin was Lord High Treasurer from May 1702 to August 1710, and Marlborough Captain-General from March 1701 until December 1711. Sarah's unique position, as the monarch's favourite and the wife and friend of two chief ministers, was the perfect platform for anyone with ambition, let alone a woman, to exercise considerable influence in the affairs of the country at this time of change. While she maintained her influence, Marlborough and Godolphin kept England committed to the 'Grand Alliance' against Louis XIV's France. Sarah's influence was such that King Charles III of Spain consulted her rather than the Queen.

Sarah was only 15 when she met and fell in love with John Churchill. Born at Holywell, St Albans on 5 June 1660, the year the monarchy was restored, Sarah accompanied her sister, Frances Jenyns, when she became a maid of honour in the household of the then Duchess of York – James's first wife, Anne Hyde, in 1673. Also attached to the household of the Duke of York was the young John Churchill, made a page to the Duke by courtesy of his sister, Arabella, who had become the Duke's mistress. Born in 1650 and from similarly modest gentry stock to Sarah, Churchill received an army commission in 1667 at the age of 17, serving initially in the English garrison at Tangier. The young Churchill became involved with one of Charles II's many mistresses, Barbara Villiers, Duchess of Cleveland. An old, and probably apocryphal, story had Charles finding Churchill hiding in a cupboard in her room, and dismissing him with the words, 'Go: you are a rascal, but I forgive you because you do it to get your bread.'[2]

It would seem from descriptions at the time that Churchill's main asset was his fine looks and 'inimitable sweetness and gentleness' of his manner.[3]

It was felt amongst his contemporaries that he was built in too delicate a manner ever to become an accomplished officer and soldier, 'the whole fabric of his body indicated nothing like strength and vigour'.[4] Despite a few petty quarrels it was soon clear that the couple were equally desirous of entering into courtship, although for a time they only met in public at balls, plays, drawing-room entertainments at Court, and in private at maids' lodgings. John Churchill relayed his true passion for her in his letters, writing that 'I love you with all my hart and soul' and 'I am never truly happy but when I am with you'.[5] After a year, Churchill made a proposal of marriage to Sarah, but to their distress his parents refused to consent to the match, having in mind Katherine, the heiress of playwright Sir Charles Sedley.

Rumours circulating about Katherine included her lack of beauty and the fact that she had a mother who had been confined in an asylum for many years. It was said that Katherine was already 'as mad as her mother, and as vicious as her father', and that the Churchills were willing to marry their eldest son 'to a shocking creature for money'.[6] John Churchill was torn between love for Sarah and duty as a son. Sarah took out her spleen on her indecisive lover in her letters, accusing him 'surely you must confess that you have been the falsest creature upon earth to me'.[7] However, their attraction for each other grew.

The death of Sarah's brother Ralph brought unexpected wealth to Sarah, which softened the resolve of Churchill's parents to the idea of their union. The couple were married in secret in late 1677. It was not publicly known until months later, when their situation was more certain, and Sarah was able to resign her post as maid of honour and announce her wedded status.

Their married life was one of constant separation. Over the next few years many of Churchill's letters were directly concerned with his wife's seemingly unshakable conviction that her husband was conducting a string of affairs. His written response being the affirmation that 'I swaire to you waire we unmaryed, I would beg you on my knees to be my wife.'[8]

By 1684, John Churchill did not hold, nor did he seem likely to hold, a ministerial appointment. His peers found the rumour that he was being considered for Secretary of State hilarious, taunting that he had yet to learn to write. His peacetime duties were ceremonial only, and he was regarded as a harmless and pleasant family man, an image that did not displease him. His letters show that he feared Sarah's displeasure and lack of affection. 'I only beg that you will love me always soe well as I love you, and then we can not but happy,' he wrote. Sarah seemed to have cultivated an air about her that fostered the opinion that she held her affection and approval in reserve, and that it had to be begged for. By this stage, they were acquiring money, whilst not excessively wealthy, and becoming what was termed 'people of substance'. For the first time they were in a position to make loans to the Exchequer. Sarah was taking control of their daily affairs and complained Churchill 'could not manage matters so as was convenient for our Circumstances, [and] this obliged me to enter into the management of my family'.[9] In most households of the time it would probably have been unthinkable for a wife to act in this way. Taking the helm and not expecting any opposition was one of Sarah's outstanding qualities.

Sarah's inheritance provided them with the wherewithal to purchase some land, the highest form of investment. They were able to acquire a country estate befitting their rank. The tragic death of Sarah's sister Barbara and her only child added her share of the wealth back into the family. This was followed by successful negotiations to buy the remaining share of the family estate, Sandridge and Holywell, for £11,000, an extortionate sum for the times. It came with a Tudor mansion near London, which needed extensive renovation. Sarah's power was sufficient to organize the diversion of a highway away from the frontage of their house, and to give it the feeling of being in the country.

The letters they exchanged whenever absent from each other demonstrate Marlborough's constant devotion to his 'dearest soul'. In one early letter, he told Sarah, 'If your happiness can depend upon the esteem and love I have for you, you ought to be the happiest thing breathing, for I have never anybody loved to that height I do you.'[10] In April 1703, after receiving two letters from Sarah when he was at The Hague, he wrote, 'I am so entirely yours, that if I might have all the world given me, I could not be happy but in your love.'[11] Notwithstanding Sarah's mercurial temperament, she did love Marlborough. In 1692 when he was in the Tower, Sarah wrote, 'Wherever you are whilst I have life, my soul shall follow you, my ever dear Lord Marl., and wherever I am I shall only kill the time, wish for night that I may sleep, and hope the next day to hear from you.'[12] Whilst he benefited greatly by his wife's interventions, Marlborough was utterly besotted with her, as his letters, while on campaigns, frequently showed: 'Good success is the only thing that can give me the blessing of ending my days quietly with you my dear soul.'[13] Lady Percy once wrote that Sarah had married Marlborough for love 'and he always made her so good a return as to deserve the continuance of her kindness'.[14] However, the well-known quotation attributed to Sarah, 'The Duke returned from the wars today and did pleasure me in his top-boots', is almost certainly apocryphal. Many years after Marlborough's death, when she received a marriage proposal from the Duke of Somerset, she replied, 'If I were young and handsome as I was, instead of old and faded as I am, and you could lay the empire of the world at my feet, you should never share the heart and hand that once belonged to John, Duke of Marlborough.'[15]

Sarah was adept at manipulating others for her own ends. Godolphin once complimented her on this as being 'the reason and understanding by which you are most justly distinguished from the rest of your sex'.[16] She had a thunderous temper, believed to have been inherited from her mother. It would come upon her 'like a fit of fever' when denied something she wished for. This was not a trait she ever fully grew out of.[17] Upon her father's death, as the last in line, it was solely her gender which prevented her succession to both her father and grandfather as MP for St Albans. For most young women this would not have been a major issue, but for Sarah it was a crippling blow, and a denial of entry into a world in which she so longed to participate. Not even Sarah could fight this particular cause, but her frustration may have been an influence upon the level of determination she threw into her future activities, as perhaps proof that anything a man could do she could do better.

Sarah was a rare being, a female with a 'passion for government',[18] one of history's other 'Iron Ladies'. She appears to have been born with an obsession to wield power. This aspect of her character owes as much to nurture as well as nature. During her childhood, Sarah's mother, Frances Jenyns, suffered extreme financial hardships as a result of her husband George Hamilton's diversion of funds she felt were rightfully hers and her children's. After his death, Frances was left to cope with a set of lawsuits in order to secure some financial stability for her young family. Sarah, growing up in a quarrelsome and insecure atmosphere, developed a fierce determination not to allow her own family to go through the ravages of such monetary disputes. This turned into a lifelong passion to fight the cause of women being able to possess financial independence.

Another disadvantage of her gender was that Sarah 'had little if any advantage from education'.[19] She devised her own system of arithmetic calculation, which was usually correct, but which looked 'as if a child had scrabbled over the paper here and there at random'. By her own admission, she hated 'writing all things . . . and never reads any book but the World'.[20] Sarah knew that to make credible inroads into the power spectrum of politics, she needed to expand her basic education. She used the tedium of her enforced leisure as an opportunity to attend to the simpler skills of reading, writing and spelling. Once on this track, she made up for lost time. She read as many works of political controversy as were available at the time, to inform her future involvement in high matters of state both at home and overseas. She broadened her choice of literature to embrace the classics, but also less common choices, particularly for a woman, including works in the genre of *The Anatomy of Melancholy*. Sarah's friends reacted with a mixture of mirth and incomprehension at the change in her.

Once attached to the Court, she became increasingly drawn to its intrigues. The only official role in public life open to women was that of professional courtier, very much in the vein of being seen and not heard. The limitations imposed by Court life were irksome to Sarah. 'I will constrain myself as much as possible,' she wrote to her friend Frances Hamilton, 'But som times it would provoke a sant.' She only tolerated her position as a means of what we now term networking, with a view to increasing her influence beyond the walls of the court out into the political arena. Extraordinarily for a girl in her teens (in her own tongue-in-cheek words, 'one of the simple sex'),[21] she began actively supporting the first of the Whigs during the so-called Exclusion Crisis of 1679–81, whereby the Whigs tried to exclude the Catholic James from succeeding his brother as king. Family precedent coloured her support of the Whigs.

She became a friend to the young Princess Anne and her confidante in the intrigues around the Court. Sarah was everything Anne was not, and soon supplanted Mary Cornwallis as Anne's favourite. Much intrigue and differing accounts surround the events leading up to Sarah's eventual position as prime confidante of Lady Anne. Sarah recorded that by 1682, after four years in the favoured spot, Mrs Cornwallis had received from Anne 'above a thousand letters full of the most violent professions of everlasting kindness. King Charles used to say, No man ever loved his Mistress, as his niece Anne did Mrs Cornwallis.' She attributed Mary Cornwallis's dismissal to 'the Duke of York's distaste for the fervid feeling between the two girls'. Quite what conclusions can be drawn from that, it is difficult to say, but Sarah went on to observe that less than a fortnight later Anne 'seem'd as perfectly to have forgot this Woman as if she had never heard of Her'.[22]

Compared to some of Sarah's more intelligent and sophisticated friends, Anne, five years younger, made a rather tedious companion. Anne's letters to her reveal her insecurities. 'I know I have a great many Rivalls which makes me feare loosing what I so much value,' she wrote.[23] She wielded her royal power, despite her longing for equality, by insisting that Sarah spent as much time as possible with her alone. Sarah had no option but to comply, as her growing power depended upon the cultivation of this crucial alliance. The universality of the joys and tragedies of motherhood, no respecter of royalty, was a continuing bond between the two women, despite the polarity of both their temperaments and political alignments.

It was to Sarah's advantage that the insecure Anne craved intense friendships and she tolerated Anne's company as a means of achieving her own aims. Sarah later suggested that Anne's friendships 'were flames of extravagant passion, ending in indifference or aversion', and that she loved 'fawning and adoration'.[24] In a later biographical account compiled by Sarah and written in the third person, she conveys the essence of the relationship:

The Duchess had address and accomplishments and confidence of her mistress without owing anything to the want of them in others. But yet this made room for her the sooner and gave her some advantage; and she now began to employ all Her wit and Her vivacity and almost all Her time to divert, and entertain, and serve, the Princess; and to fix that favour, which now one might easily observe to be increasing towards her every day. This favour quickly became a passion; and a Passion which possessed the Heart of the Princess too much to be hid. They were shut up together for many hours daily. Every moment of Absence was counted a sort of tedious, lifeless state. To see the Duchess was a constant joy; and to part with her for never so short a time, a constant Uneasiness; As the Princess's own frequent expressions were. This worked even to the jealousy of a Lover. She used to say she desired to possess her wholly; and could hardly bear that she should ever escape, from this confinement, into other Company.[25]

Following Anne's marriage in 1683 to Prince George, the King of Denmark's brother, John Churchill encouraged Sarah to offer her services in the newly-organized Court. Sarah's dislike of Court life held her back initially, but once she saw that there were many who opposed her in such a favoured position, the value of it increased. 'My Lord Rochester wanted to have one in my place that would be intirely obedient to him; which he had experienced I would not be,' Sarah wrote.[26] She began to view such a position, despite the servitude and low salary it carried, as being the perfect way to gain royal influence and favour, not only for herself but for her husband and family. Anne had been under pressure by those around her not to appoint Sarah, favouring ladies of more mature years and sober experience. Anne wrote to her promising 'I will try once more be he never so angry . . . I am sure you have not a faithfuller friend on earth that loves you better than I do.'[27] Sarah was eventually offered the post. She recognized the life she had in Court as the only way that a woman such as herself could wield power to secure her family's advancement and extend her influence beyond the walls of the Court and out into the wider political arena. She became the thorn in the side of many men whose aspirations had been to exert such power.

In the weeks following the dramatic escape from Whitehall in 1688, it was Sarah's negotiations which laid the foundations for future events.

She was well aware of the danger to herself of having such a hold over the Princess. She admitted to being 'fearful about everything the Princess did, when she was *thought to be advised by me*'.[28] Sarah was at the helm of discussions over such weighty issues as Anne's precedence to the throne in favour of her brother-in-law, William. Anne's sister Mary recalled at the time, 'I saw plainly that she was so absolutely governed by Lady Marlborough that it was to no purpose to intervene.'[29] Sarah resented the continuing situation of being held solely to blame for many of Anne's decisions, and encouraged Anne to warm towards her sister, even though it may seem as if she were cooling towards herself.

Sarah and Marlborough had favoured Anne's claim to the throne over that of William and Mary, and such was Sarah's closeness with Anne that she pressed her to seek a greater annual income than William was initially prepared to offer. As a result of this, Anne secured £50,000 per annum and, in turn, she increased Sarah's annual court income from £400 to £1,400 per annum.(in modern currency about £185,000.) Despite this, Sarah began to find life at Court less than pleasant. She attracted displeasure from William and Mary, which reflected on her husband's career path, and her salary she considered insufficient to sustain her desired lifestyle.

She began to think that, with Anne unlikely to outlive her sister Mary, her position held less and less advantage. It seemed likely that Anne suspected Sarah's discontent, for she wrote to offer her an extra £1,000 per year, arguing that it was as thanks for Sarah's part in securing her increased revenue. Sarah accepted, justifying her acceptance as an obligation to her struggling family purse. This friendship appears to have been more intense from Anne's perspective. She attempted to create equality between them, but at best it was illusory; Sarah was the dominant force. She did feel genuine affection for Anne, but her first priority was always the opportunities the close alliance gave her.

In an attempt by Anne to set their friendship on equal terms, the quaint custom began of them writing to each other as 'Mrs Morley' (Anne) and 'Mrs Freeman' (Sarah). Princess Anne was never happy for Sarah to be away from her, saying 'I shall be at no ease until I am in your arms.'[30] There is little doubt that Sarah monopolised Anne's friendship, and her influence was noticed by all who had dealings with the Court. Sarah, however, felt constrained by her position.

Sarah's position as favourite at Court and her easy friendship and sharing gossip with those close to her, often proved dangerous for her husband's career, causing him at times to pay the price for Sarah's intrigues. Rumours caused William to suspect that there was a more serious conspiracy against him than was the case.[31] As a consequence, without notice on 20 January 1692, Marlborough was dismissed from all his posts, with no official reason given. The King spread it around that Marlborough had been discovered in discussion with the Jacobites, added to which it was rumoured that Sarah had betrayed certain secret plans against France. The King was offended by Marlborough's criticism of his promoting foreigners to senior military positions, and he no longer wished to put up with Sarah's meddling. Sarah reluctantly admitted that perhaps she had spoken a little too freely in company she now knew to be untrustworthy, but insisted that it was 'nothing that ought to have done the Duke of Marlborough any prejudice'.[32]

Sarah was expected to resign, but nothing could have been further from her mind. For two weeks she kept away from Court, but was persuaded to return by friends, who thought that shirking her duty of attending Anne may give greater power to those wishing to dismiss her. Sarah accompanied Anne on her next visit to Kensington. In William and Mary's subsequent fury, despite Anne's pleas, they insisted that the Lord Chamberlain order Sarah to leave her post and the accommodation that went with it. Sarah was forced to leave Court, but in an extraordinary display of spirit, so as to retain Sarah's services, Anne made the decision to move to Sion House, Brentford, a residence over which the Lord Chamberlain had no jurisdiction. She begged Sarah to go with her, saying 'I had rather live in a cottage with you then reinge Emporess of the world without you.'[33]

To keep her pride intact, Sarah insisted it be known that she had offered her resignation, but that it had been refused. In these difficult times, Sarah could not forgo her own substantial salary, nor the only foothold the Marlboroughs had at court. It was Sarah's unquelled ambition for herself and her husband which was her driving force in a situation many would have considered hopeless. At Sion House, Sarah's position was not without difficulty. Anne's household, including her husband Prince George, were resentful of the isolation they now faced, plus the implications of the possible withdrawal of Anne's income. Prince George was under pressure to persuade Anne to let Sarah go. Sarah pondered the wisdom of staying close to Anne, but Anne, always determined over matters which threatened to deprive her of 'one of the greatest comforts of my life', would hear of no such thing.[34]

In a desperate attempt to be rid of Sarah, Lord Nottingham was ordered to make public a declaration to the effect that Sarah had stored up so much trouble between the Queen and Anne, that she deserved 'Her Majesties displeasure'.[35] There was no lower regard than to be viewed as such. The Queen followed suit by forbidding all members of her own court to visit the Princess, insinuating not only disgrace, but suspicion of treachery. The situation worsened when Marlborough was arrested as a suspected Jacobite, and committed to the Tower accused of high treason. Sarah was only allowed access to him by being willing to share his imprisonment, but he urged her to stay with the Princess, hoping that there might still be some advantage in doing so. Tragically, at this time, the Marlboroughs' young son Charles was taken ill and died. Marlborough's attempt to gain his release was unsuccessful, and he was due for indictment for high treason. Sarah had to shoulder the burden of her personal grief amidst the politics which threatened to bring the household to ruin. The Princess wrote to her between her visits, 'For God's sake have a care for your dear self . . . and give as little way to melancholy thoughts as you can.'[36]

The allegations against Marlborough were discovered to have been false, and following his release the family resided mainly at their St Albans home. Although she retained her official post in Anne's household, Sarah's visits to the Princess, then living in Bath, became less frequent. Despite her high profile in public life over recent years, she withdrew from such involvements and kept herself in the background. For a while it seemed that the domestic life suited both Sarah and her husband. They organized a garden which supplied their household with food, and kept a cow for a constant provision of dairy needs. By the end of 1694, it seemed as if the chances of the Marlboroughs re-entering public life were negligible, but unforeseen events are often those which change the course of history.

Queen Mary was struck down with smallpox. In response to Anne's request to visit her, the King discouraged her, but sent a message of thanks with assurance that she would be welcome to come should the Queen recover. The Queen did not, and upon her death, Anne sent William a letter of condolence, asking to visit him. There followed a slow reconciliation between William and Anne, which favoured Sarah, as William showed none of the Queen's desire to be rid of her. By 1698, largely due to his wife's continuing influence, Marlborough was restored to favour.

Sarah spent most of her time devoted to the upbringing of her remaining family. Her days with Anne, now next in line to the throne, were as tedious as they had ever been, but she was ever mindful of its potential advantages, admitting 'I have gone a thousand times to her when I had rather have been in a dungeon.'[37] King William was not in good health, and during this period, the Marlboroughs and Godolphin, greatly assisted by Sarah's influence, laid the foundations to slip easily into the role of Anne's chief confidential advisers, once she inherited the throne.

It did not take long for Anne to consult them unfailingly before taking any decision, great or small, heralding a change in fortunes which had hitherto seemed inconceivable. Sarah's hold over Anne's affection was great enough to be granted funds to enhance the dower packages of her daughters to make them more desirable matches. William, aware of such decisions 'fell into a great passion', accusing Anne of acting as if she were 'Queen before her time'.[38]

In July 1701 Marlborough finally got his desired military position as commander-in-chief of 10,000 men to aid the Dutch, and to form an alliance with other European powers to oppose the French. Sarah was determined to join him at The Hague as soon as possible, with her young family, welcoming the opportunity to leave the boredom and restrictions of many years dominated by life in Court circles. However, Sarah's lack of tolerance of foreign etiquette and customs caused her to be bad-tempered with those around her, often with those she would have been well advised to seek to impress. Marlborough found her behaviour unpredictable and less than polite, and when he succeeded in getting her back to England in October, she was never again allowed to accompany him abroad in an official capacity.

King William died on 8 March 1702. Europe was on the brink of a major war, and Anne succeeded as Queen. She was sadly lacking in the skills required to lead the country, and Sarah's long and reluctantly devoted friendship finally came into its own, and paid the dividends that had always been sought. Marlborough was made a Knight of the Garter. For Sarah, it seemed, no request could be refused. Her appointment as Keeper of the Royal Purse gave her useful control over the Queen's personal spending money. Sarah's income, entirely separate from that of her husband, was over £6,000 per year, a handsome amount to add to her existing fortune. It was in Sarah's gift to fill subordinate posts, which she had no qualms about bestowing upon her own servants and family. This situation caused much resentment, and Sarah may have been better advised to grant at least a few favours beyond her own circle of interest. She was reported to have been rude and discourteous to those who sought positions for which she had already decided the outcomes. She was aware of the dissension she caused and knew that 'there were but few Women that would not have poysond me for the Happynesse they thought I enjoyed'.[39]

Marlborough was elevated to his dukedom shortly after Anne succeeded to the throne in March 1702. Sarah was elevated to Groom of the Stole, Mistress of the Robes and Controller of the Privy Purse, her income now in excess of £6,000 a year with an annual grant of £2,000 a year from the Privy Purse. The renewed, and at times fragile, intimacy with Queen Anne ensured the opportunity for Marlborough and Godolphin to become established as her confidential advisers. Throughout the partnership Sarah expected to be given all the letters Marlborough had written to Godolphin, even claiming the right to open and read them first if they arrived while Godolphin was absent. Godolphin reminded Marlborough frequently that nothing could be kept from her.[40]

Marlborough, Godolphin, Sarah and the Queen formed a close unit, the common factor uniting them being Sarah. Marlborough's favour was primarily due to the fact that he was 'Mrs Freeman's husband', rather than his own abilities. Sarah's position was an asset in his dealings with foreign affairs, as he was deemed to have the complete confidence of the Queen, due the closeness of his wife to the Royal ear, even when he was out of the country. Anne may have realized that, without this support, she would have been a vulnerable and inadequate monarch.

Sarah's political involvement has been described as one of 'passionate wrong-headedness, of an arrogant, driven, opinionated woman . . . as often as not damaging the very cause she wished to promote'. Sarah, impervious to the opinions of many who surrounded her, boasted in old age that 'no woman had ever been so useful to her family'.[41] Her friendship and favour with Queen Anne was the catalyst for the spectacular European career of her husband, which trickled along and down the familial line.

Sarah was the driving force behind building and furnishing houses, including Blenheim Palace. She invested capital and bought estates. At times some of those closest to her may have felt overwhelmed by the sheer force of her personality. She was admired, feared and hated in equal measure.

Sarah had not tiptoed through the world in order to get her own way. By her own admission she referred to confrontation as 'a perpetual warr' with the fools who surrounded her. She never acquired the gift of tactfully controlling her tongue, or allowing others any sort of control over her. It would have been a brave being who dared to criticise her. She placed high value on what she termed her 'devastating sincerity',[42] even when she knew the dreadful consequences.

Sarah's influence could be seen in many ways. On 8 September 1705 Lord Sutherland, then envoy at Vienna, wrote quite openly to the Duchess of appointments and sackings: 'The other remove you mention will be a very fortunate thing, for believe me, nobody has done more mischief than that person.'[43] He often used Sarah as a means of persuading the Queen to comply with his wishes after he became Secretary of State in 1706. The Queen regularly acted upon matters brought to her notice by Sarah, as in the case of a libeller called Stephens, despite her misgivings. She wrote in June 1706: 'I have upon my dear Mrs Freeman's pressing letter about Mr Stephens, ordered Mr Secretary Harley to put a stop to his standing in the pillory, till further orders, which is in effect the same thing as if he was pardoned. Nothing but your desire could have inclined me to it; for, in my opinion, it is not right.'[44]

Marlborough, too, was often swayed by his wife's opinion as to who obtained favours conferred. In June 1706 he wrote, 'I am so much of your opinion that I do assure you Lord Feversham's nephews shall never be recommended by me for the favour of the Queen.'[45] He consulted Sarah on all matters including approving offices, where to keep horses, or what tapestries to buy. He wrote 'I am to have a set of horses from the Elector of Hanover. Shall I bring them over or keep them here as you shall think best? A set of hangings is at Antwerp bespoken by the late King. Would you have me buy them? They have neither silver nor gold.'[46] Due to her self-exalted and influential position, there were those who feared Sarah, and strove to ingratiate themselves with her. Those under her influence felt it was more important to obey, and be in the good grace of Sarah than it was of the Queen, such was her ability to alter the course of their lives for better or for worse.

Among Sarah's protégés was Charles Mordaunt, 3rd Earl of Peterborough, commander of English and Dutch forces in Spain in April 1705. He was effusive in his letters: 'You cannot imagine Madame, how much the dependence on your protection has given my heart in the greatest difficulties, and I flatter myself so far as to think I may hope for the continuence of your friendship, which I value at the highest rate, and shall endeavour by all means in my power to preserve.'[47] Some wrote long letters to her to justify why she may have thought badly of them, such as the Whig polemicist, Arthur Maynwaring, in April 1708 'I am afraid I shall lose your Grace's patience, but I hope you won't think of troubling yourself to answer this letter, though I can't help writing it, because there is something in your last that looks as if what I had said had implied that I thought your Grace had been in the wrong. I am very uneasy under this apprehension.'[48]

By 1706 there were growing signs that the Queen was becoming somewhat peeved with Sarah's imperious attitude. In July 1706 Anne wrote to Sarah: 'You wronged me very much in thinking that I am influenced by some you mention in disposing of church preferments. Ask those whom I am sure you will believe, though you won't me, and they can tell you I never disposed of any without advising them. I have upon this that you fancy to have so much power with me.'[49] Sarah's rely to Anne was typical of her extraordinary insensitivity to the Queen's status: 'Your Majesty's great indifference and contempt in taking no notice of my last letter did not so much surprise me as to hear my Lord Treasurer [Godolphin] say you had complained much of it, which makes me presume to give you this trouble to repeat what I can be very positive was the whole aim of the letter, and I believe very near the words.'[50] Anne could see that her own power was in the process of being eclipsed by Sarah's, and desired the situation to return to that of earlier years. She wrote again to Sarah a few days later: 'I shall dine at St James's and shall be very glad to see you there, and be assured whenever you will be the same to me as you was five years ago, you shall find me the same tender faithful Morley.'[51]

Ironically, it was Sarah's continued use of royal patronage as a means of advancing the careers of other members of her family that was to bring about her downfall. She had earlier found appointments for her cousin Jack Hill as a groom of the bedchamber and his sister Alice as a laundress when both their parents had died. In 1704, she found a position for the eldest Hill sister, Abigail, as bedchamber woman to the Queen. Abigail was obviously meant to spare Sarah some of the burden of entertaining Anne. Sarah probably felt a sense of having done good for a less-fortunate branch of her family, but this decision was to prove crucial to the events over the following years. Abigail, thrilled with her appointment, proved herself a faithful and discreet servant, something of a rarity in the court, and Anne soon took a particular liking to the young woman.

Abigail's elder brother was also in need of a good word and financial support, but Sarah, preferring to use her influence rather than her purse, referred the young man to relatives of her father, the Harleys. Under normal circumstances an approach for help such as this may well have been refused but it was becoming known that to curry favour with Sarah, Duchess of Marlborough, was a wise move, given her elevated position in court. So it was that a bond between Abigail, and her cousin, the aspiring politician, Robert Harley, and the Hills was created that would prove highly significant.

Unfortunately, Sarah was too blinkered to understand that for her position to be maintained, it was necessary for her to remain on obsequiously good terms with the Queen, rather than sacrifice her goodwill in order to achieve her own political aspirations. Her stubborn attitude eventually alienated the Queen, not accustomed to being challenged or criticised. In a strange twist of events, the Queen was to transfer her affections to Abigail, placed in her path by Sarah in an act of kindness towards a less fortunate family member. The Queen's displeasure did not end with Sarah, but also dispelled her confidence in her two ministers. This loss of favour brought joy to the hearts of rival influences at Court, who seized the chance to use their powers to such an extent that this rift was in hindsight judged by the Whigs to have been instrumental in bringing about their downfall.

Relations between Sarah and Anne were showing signs of strain as early as 1704, at the time of Marlborough's greatest victory at Blenheim. Marlborough scribbled a pencilled message to Sarah on the back of a tavern bill: 'I have no time to say more but to beg you will give my duty to the Queen and let her know her army has had a glorious victory.'[52] It reached Sarah at St James's on 21 August, at which point she immediately set out to find the Queen at Windsor. Sarah had been staying away from court with Anne complaining, 'everything I say is imputed either to partiality or being imposed upon by knaves and fools'.[53]

By this time, Abigail Hill was supplanting Sarah in the Queen's affections. Sarah complained to the Queen in July 1707 that Abigail 'is one occation of feeding Mrs Morley's passions for the torrys by taking all occations to speake well of some of them, & by giving you a prejudice to those that are truly in your interest'.[54] As Sarah became more troublesome to the Queen, so Abigail became more agreeable. Sarah was slow to recognize the danger, even when Anne wrote back to her in July 1707, taking issue with Sarah's complaints about Abigail, 'therefore I shall only, in the first place, beg your pardon once more for what I said the other day, which I find you take ill; and say something in answer to your explanation of the suspicions you seemed to have concerning your cousin Hill, who is very far from being an occasion of feeding Mrs Morley in her passion, as you are pleased to call it; she never meddling with anything'.[55]

Marlborough was fully alive to the dangers posed by Abigail, warning Sarah that 'you can't oblige Abigail more than by being at a distance with [The Queen]'.[56] Writing to Sarah in April 1708, Maynwaring understood how the Queen's new allegiance might affect the political allies of Marlborough and Godolphin: 'Though your Grace seems to think that kindness once gone never returns, I think it is plain that there is still a great unwillingness to break quite with your Grace . . . Therefore for God's sake, Madam, come to court again and be assured, nothing will so much dark the hopes of your enemies, nothing will so please or revive your friends.'

Sarah then learned that Abigail had married Samuel Masham, a gentleman of Prince George's household, and that the Queen herself had attended the secret ceremony. Oblivious to the harm she was doing to her own position, Sarah confronted Anne. In July 1708 she accused Anne of a 'strange and unaccountable' passion for Abigail, implying they were lesbian lovers. It reflected the allegations being circulated. Sarah had failed to understand that Anne had kept the wedding secret through fear of her reaction and that the Queen still craved affection. All she received was Sarah's hectoring.[57]

Abigail's cousin, Robert Harley, was beginning to separate himself from the war policies of Godolphin and Marlborough and display more overtly Tory sympathies. The Whigs distrusted Harley and had advanced Sunderland, with Sarah's connivance, precisely to begin to eject Harley from office. Harley attempted to continue his efforts with the Queen's backing, and used Abigail's growing influence over Anne during the crisis. Marlborough was increasingly aware of the threat Abigail posed, writing to Sarah in August 1708, 'The account you give me of the commerce and kindness of the Queen to Mrs Masham is that which will at last bring all things to ruin; for by all you write I see the Queen is determined to support, and, I believe, at last own her.'[58]

In a desperate attempt to discredit the Queen's relationship with Abigail, Sarah passed the Queen's letters around. Marlborough sensed the risks, writing in May 1708, 'I believe Lord Treasurer [Godolphin] and you are of opinion with me, that the Queen should not know that her letters are sent to anybody.' He also suggested that, 'when the Queen is sensible of her being ill advised, she will then readily agree to all that may be advised by Lord Treasurer, myself, and you. I pray God it may not then be too late!'[59] Similarly, on 19 August 1709, Marlborough noted, 'I shall say very little to you concerning the Queen, who is by no means obliging; but if you can't regain her affections that matter will continue as it now is. I would go up on all fours to make it easy between you, but for credit I am satisfied I have none so that willingly I would not expose myself, but meddle as little as possible.'[60] Three days later, Marlborough reassured Sarah of his love, 'I see by it that the Queen continues her cold and unkind proceeding towards you; that must be, so long as Mrs Masham has the opportunities of being daily with her. Be obliging and kind to all my friends and avoid entering into cabals, and whatever I have in this world, if that can give you any satisfaction, you shall always be mistress of, and have the disposing of that and me.'[61]

Sarah totally disregarded Marlborough's advice, and persistently pursued her confrontational course. Matters reached a climax in the wake of Marlborough's victory at Oudenarde in July 1708. Annoyed by the Queen for not wearing the jewels she had laid out for her in her role as Mistress of the Robes for the celebration on 19 August 1708 of the victory, Sarah publicly told the Queen to be quiet on the steps of St Paul's. She finally realized that she had stepped beyond the tolerance of the Queen, and attempted some explanation in forwarding a letter from Marlborough expressing his loyalty to the Queen. Anne replied curtly on 22 August, 'After the commands you gave me in the church, on the thanksgiving, of not answering you, I should not have troubled you with these lines, but to return the Duke of Marlborough's letter safe into your hands, and for the same reason do not say anything to that, nor to yours which enclosed it.'[62] Having learned of the disastrous situation, Marlborough admitted that he thought the Queen had been made jealous of his own power, and that nothing they could now do would bring about a reconciliation: 'This villainy has been insinuated by Mrs Masham by the instigation of Harley, who certainly is the worst of men.'[63]

Marlborough never truly castigated Sarah for her lack of wisdom concerning her relationship with Anne. Fixated by his desire to please his wife, he dwelt once more on the practicalities of finishing Blenheim Palace, where he longed to be with her at the earliest opportunity. He wrote in July 1709, 'I hope the alterations you have made in the ceilings will not hinder the finishing of your apartment and mine so that we may finish it next spring. Am glad of the general applause your house meets with, since I am sure it gives you pleasure; and for the same reason be not uneasy that it costs more money than you thought it would for upon my word, I shall think nothing too much for the making you easy.'[64]

Sarah was not without all influence, but Maynwaring was alert to the growing adverse public perception of her, writing in October 1709, 'I desire you not to trouble or concern yourself of what is said of you, tis all old and incredible stuff of extortion and affairs with Godolphin and Shrewsbury, which not a soul living believes a word of; and there is one scene which I think you could hardly help laughing at; which is, when you are going to be pulled to pieces by the mob for all manner of ill done to the Queen and England.'[65] It was only the Queen's fear that Marlborough might resign that kept Sarah in her posts.

Marlborough advised Sarah to stay away from Court and neither confront Anne nor ask for favours. But, true to type, Sarah ignored his counsel, writing with incredible frankness to Anne:

> I can't help renewing my request that you will explain without the trouble of writing a long answer to this, what it is that prevails with you to oppose the advice of all your old servants and councils, – if it be not that woman and those that apply to you by her . . . To shew you that I am not alone of this opinion, if I should ask the first ordinary man that I met what had caused so great a change in you, he would say that the reason was because you were grown very fond of Mrs Masham, and were governed by those that govern her. And now because you pray to God to open my eyes, I will say how you may do that to yourself if you please, for this would open my eyes and everybody's else.[66]

Sarah was never once able to understand both the audacity and folly of this type of approach to the Queen. The letter elicited the following reply on 26 October 1709, 'I know this place is reckoned under your office; but there is no office whatsoever that has the entire disposal of anything under them; but I may put in any one I please, when I have a mind to it.'[67]

In March 1710, Sarah made it known that if England left the war, she would resign her offices in favour of her two daughters, Lady Sunderland and Lady Rialton, claiming the Queen had promised this previously. When Sarah sought assurances, the Queen remarked that she did not recall and 'I desire that I may never be troubled any more on the subject'.[68] Amid rumours that Sarah had been openly criticising her, Anne managed to avoid seeing Sarah for several days. Sarah asked for an audience in a letter in which she wrote, 'What I have to say in my own vindication will have no consequence in obliging her Majesty to answer.' Anne picked up on the phrase, repeating it over and over again when Sarah finally met her on 6 April 1710, 'You desired no answer, and you shall have none.' Anne was also adamant that anything Sarah had to say must be put in writing. This culminated in the most famous, and final, interaction between Sarah and her monarch, Queen Anne, when Sarah visited her on Good Friday, 6 April 1710:

> As soon as I open the door she said she was going to write to me.
>   'Upon what Madame?' said I.
> Queen: I did not open your letter till just now and I was going to write to you.
> Duchess: Was there anything in it Madam that you had a mind to answer?
> Queen: I think there is nothing you can have to say, but you can write it.
> Duchess: Won't your Majesty give me leave to tell it to you?
> Queen: Whatever you have to say you may write it.
> Duchess: Indeed I can't tell how to put such sort of things into writing.
> Queen: You may put it into writing.
> Duchess: Won't your Majesty allow me to tell it you now I am here?
> Queen: You may put it into writing.

Duchess: I believe your Majesty never did so hard thing to anybody, as to refuse to hear them speak, even the meanest person than ever desired it.

Queen: Yes, I do bid people to put what they have to say in writing, when I have a mind to it.

Duchess: I have nothing to say, madam, upon the subject that is so uneasy to you; that person is not, that I know of, at all concerned in the account that I would give you, which I can't be quiet till I have told you.

Queen: You may put it into writing.

This continued until the Queen finally said 'I will go out of the room', which reduced the Duchess to tears, a rare occurrence. Sarah pleaded, 'I am confident your Majesty will suffer for such an instance of humanity.'

Anne replied, 'That will be to myself.' They were the last words that passed between them.[69]

Sarah wrote again in June 1710, pleading with Anne,

I hope your Majesty will forgive me if I can't help troubling you once more, because it really seems to me, that nobody speaks to you at this time so freely as I should do, if it might have been allowed me; nor represents sufficiently the consequences of what you are doing . . . Therefore, pray, madam, consider seriously what you are doing, and what a precipice you are going upon . . . It is not for me to say but I once more beg your Majesty, for God's sake, to have a care what you do . . . I hope you will no longer let it be in the power of others to mortify so old and good a servant. And for God's sake, madam, what is that you would do all this for?[70]

There was no reply.

Sarah's tragedy had been to be undermined by her own weaknesses, not least her inability to curb a sharp tongue. Marlborough's Chaplain-General, Dr Francis Hare, later Bishop of both St Asaph and also of Chichester, put it delicately in writing to Sarah after her fall from grace, 'the sincerity and openness of your Grace's temper makes you not easily suspect others, and by that means, I fear the freedom of conversation your Grace has used with some persons, has been often betrayed to your great prejudice, and a very ill use has been made, by help of a little misrepresentation, of that where no ill at all was meant'.[71] She was impervious to the need to display tact towards those who wielded nominal power. She failed to see that Anne's elevation to the throne had changed the nature of the earlier relationship, for a Queen could not be seen to take political advice from a female servant: due deference should have been observed towards the Queen's status. Only later did Sarah admit, 'Dissembling is so great a force to my nature that I could never bring myself to it. Perhaps by doing it I might have prevented a great many mischiefs that have happened to me.'[72]

Ultimately, it was Sarah's dramatic loss of her position at Court through the excesses of her own character that brought about the downfall of Marlborough and Godolphin, and effectively spelled the beginning of the end of British participation in the war. Following the final disintegration of Sarah's friendship with the Queen, the only two who stood by her, despite the devastation this rift caused, were Marlborough and Godolphin, whose own political careers suffered incalculable losses as a result. Their love for her triumphed over these shadows brought about by her wilful and selfish actions over many years. Hostility to the war was being fed by military failures and increasingly high taxation. The victory of Malplaquet had been very costly and there was no further success. Allegations of Marlborough's corruption, a bad harvest, and violent religious and political controversies culminated in sweeping Tory electoral gains at the polls in 1710. Godolphin was dismissed as Lord Treasurer on 7 August 1710, with Harley, soon to be Earl of Oxford, replacing him. Godolphin paid the price of choosing friendship with Sarah over and above saving his own ministry. She did understand what it had cost him, referring to him as 'the truest friend to me . . . and the best man that ever lived'. This may have stung the poor Duke who had learnt over the years that 'a man must bear with a good deal to be quiet at home'.[73] Godolphin died in September 1712 while at the Marlborough's house in St Albans.

Marlborough did not seem to have expected Godolphin's demise, and counselled Sarah 'to keep out of the way. For nothing would please them more that wish us ill, than to have a pretext for removing of you, which to me would be a much greater mortification than any other personal thing to myself.'[74] Sarah lost her posts on 18 January 1711, and Marlborough was finally dismissed on 31 December 1711. Marlborough had some difficulty in preventing Sarah from removing the marble chimneypieces from her apartments in St James's Palace: she did remove the locks and mirrors.

When Anne died in 1714, Marlborough was restored to his post and honours by King George I. The greatest tragedy of Anne's life had been the loss of twelve children through miscarriage or stillbirth, four who survived birth, but died in infancy and one son who died when aged eleven. The next available Protestant heir, George, Elector of Hanover, was the maternal grandson of James I's daughter, Elizabeth Stuart. Predictably perhaps, Sarah did not get on with the new Princess of Wales, who was as strong willed as she was. Marlborough suffered a massive stroke in May 1715, dying on 15 June 1722.

There had never been space in Sarah's crowded life for what might be termed leisure activities, and religion contrasted too sharply with her desire to control. She may at one time have been able to control the Queen to some extent, but God was too vast a prospect, best left to others. She could only accept compliance and agreement as testaments of love for her. Nothing less satisfied, although these qualities that she demanded were a world away from what she gave to others, including the Queen and her own devoted husband. Family relationships suffered, including those with her children and grandchildren. She threatened disinheritance of her grandsons over their political misconduct.

As widow, however, Sarah went from strength to strength, investing her late husband's fortune in land and securities. An endowment to one of her grandsons procured another independent branch of her family to flourish following her death. Unusually for a dowager with male heirs of age, Sarah kept hold of the reins of her family, retaining her position as undisputed head. Her financial control was so vast that she was able to influence government interest rates. By the time of her death, Sarah was the richest woman in her own right in all of England, holding sway over twenty-seven estates in twelve counties worth over £400,000 with an annual rental income of £17,000. In addition, she had capital stock of £250,000, and £12,100 in annuities.[75]

Sarah never gave up on her political interests, using her contacts to oppose the rise of Robert Walpole, who had once been Marlborough's clerk, and who she felt did not acknowledge sufficiently the debt the Whigs owed to her and Marlborough. She became the 'immortal, undecaying toast' of those opposing Walpole.[76] She was particularly active during the 1734 election, in the unfulfilled hopes that Walpole would finally lose office.

Sarah lived for twenty-two years after Marlborough's death, devoting herself to his memory and to the continuing construction of Blenheim. She had never entertained Marlborough's grander vision of Blenheim, and there were endless disputes with the architect, Vanbrugh, as the project came in late and over budget. Sarah remained the matriarch of her family, quarrelling with her surviving daughters, all but one of whom predeceased her.

Sarah's main significance on the political stage had been transmitted through her male associates, rather than her identity as 'Mrs Freeman' to the Queen's 'Mrs Morley'. This was not the premise she had set out with during her teens. She railed against the sense of insignificance as a woman in the world of affairs, although deep down she may have appreciated the power she did hold. She appeared to have had every good fortune that life could bestow on one human being. She was likened, even to those who despised her as an 'elemental, destructive and unstoppable force of nature'.[77] She was dubbed by an enemy as 'Mount Aetna', sweeping all who stood in her way to destruction. Although those who stood most in between herself and Queen Anne proved slippery and difficult to manoeuvre around.

Confined to her bed in her later years, she still possessed the same drive and energy. No one was able to supplant her or to wrest power from her bony hands. A friend commented it looked 'as if the maker had designed both (body and mind) to be immortal, had he not been engaged to the contrary'.[78] By her own admission she wrote. 'I am confydent I should have been the greatest Hero that was ever known in the Parliament Hous, if I had been so happy as to have been a Man.' Her lifelong lament?: 'Things that are worth naming will ever be done from the influence of men.'[79]

Sarah died on 18 October 1744, being laid to rest at Blenheim alongside Marlborough, whose body was transferred from Westminster Abbey.

Chapter 2

'She Has Grown Ugly': Catherine 'Kitty' Pakenham

In March 1805 Major General Sir Arthur Wellesley arrived back in England after nine years in India. The celebrated victor over the Maratha Confederacy at the Battle of Assaye in September 1803, Wellesley had departed for India as an unknown lieutenant colonel of the 33rd Foot. Following participation in a brief and abortive military expedition to Germany and his election as MP for Rye, Wellesley crossed to Dublin in April 1806 to marry the young woman he had not seen since 1795. Reputedly, Wellesley is said to have remarked to his brother Gerald, 'She's grown ugly, by Jove.'[1] Wellesley had been determined to marry the Hon. Catherine 'Kitty' Pakenham since he had first proposed to her in 1792. But he had been rejected repeatedly as unsuitable by her family. Rejection was a turning point for Wellesley. Formerly passionately interested in music, he apparently burned his violin – some suggested he simply gave it away – vowing never to take it up again, and resolved to devote himself fully to the military profession. Writing to Kitty in June 1794, Wellesley told her that if his circumstances changed for the better in the eyes of her family then he would still want her:

> As Lord Longford's [Kitty's brother] determination is founded upon prudential motives and may be changed should my situation be altered before I return to Ireland, I hope you will believe that should anything occur which may induce you and him to change your minds, my mind will still remain the same.[2]

This rejection was the catalyst which set Wellesley on the road to military greatness.

Born in January 1772, Catherine 'Kitty' Dorothea Sarah Pakenham was the second of nine children of the wealthy landowner and naval officer, the 2nd Lord Longford. Kitty was born at the family seat of Pakenham Hall in County Westmeath. Unlike Arthur Wellesley, she came from a loving family background. Slim and small, Kitty was lively, intelligent and generous, but also impulsive and prone to gossip and indiscretion. She wrote verse, painted, and played the harp and piano. The 'Longford Lilly' was widely admired in Dublin society. She soon attracted the attention of the ADC to the Viceroy, Captain the Hon. Arthur Wesley – Wellesley was adopted as their surname by Arthur and his brothers in 1798. Kitty later said she had first seen Arthur when she was 15 and loved him from the first moment she saw him.[3]

Born in 1769, Wellesley was a son of the 1st Earl of Mornington but as the third surviving son could not hope to inherit, although he had become MP for Trim in the Irish Parliament in 1790. The family was in financial difficulties and much would depend upon the ability of Wellesley's elder brother, Richard, now 2nd Earl of Mornington, in rebuilding fortune and reputation. Richard was able to purchase Arthur's steps in rank for him and to secure the position with the Viceroy. Arthur, however, had earned a reputation for not being serious and for enjoying life in Dublin a little too much. He gambled and was fined for brawling. As a child he had been considered undistinguished compared to Richard and had performed poorly at school. His mother deemed Arthur fit only for a military career and he was packed off to the Royal Academy of Equitation in Angers on the Loire, then the capital of the French province of Anjou. He became an Ensign in the 73rd (Highland) Foot in March 1787, Richard purchasing the commission for him.

To Lord Longford, Arthur's prospects looked poor and he turned Arthur's proposal to Kitty down in early 1792. Longford died in June 1792, but his son, Thomas, now 3rd Lord Longford, was equally set against Arthur, even though Arthur purchased successively with Richard's help a lieutenancy in the 76th Foot, exchanging into the 41st Foot rather than going to India in 1788, before then transferring again to the 12th Light Dragoons. Richard had then purchased Arthur a captaincy in the 58th Foot in 1791. Thomas lectured Arthur on the need to improve his character. Ironically, Thomas Longford was younger than both Arthur and Kitty, and it can be imagined how galling Arthur found it to be lectured by a younger man who, as head of the family, had the right of veto. After a transfer to the 18th Light Dragoons, and once more with Richard's assistance, Arthur secured a majority in the 33rd Foot in April 1793 and then the lieutenant colonelcy of the 33rd Foot in September 1793.

Arthur managed to purchase a regiment at the age of only 24, but Thomas's younger brother, Edward, had been a lieutenant colonel at 17, so when Arthur proposed again in 1794 he was rejected once more. Thus it was that Arthur wrote to Kitty in June 1794 promising to remain faithful to his intention to marry her. Kitty was forbidden by her brother and mother to communicate with Arthur at all. Arthur returned to Dublin after campaigning with his regiment in Flanders and did meet Kitty in public on occasions, but the embargo on written communications remained, as did his barring from Pakenham Hall. Arthur was all but ready to give up his commission when his regiment was ordered to India in June 1796.

In Arthur's absence, Kitty was wooed by another young officer, Galbraith Lowry Cole, a younger son of the Earl of Enniskillen, who was on the staff of the Commander-in-Chief in Ireland, but it was Arthur she still loved. News of Arthur's successes in India and his improving finances on active service – not least from prize money from the capture of Indian fortresses – were instrumental in Kitty turning down Lowry Cole's proposal of marriage in early 1801. There seems to have been a brief engagement between Kitty and Lowry Cole and the strain on Kitty may have resulted in something of a nervous breakdown.[4] By the time he came home Arthur had amassed about £43,000, a process assisted by his brother, Richard, becoming Governor General of India in 1798 and elevated to Marquis Wellesley in the following year

Unable to write directly to each other, Kitty and Arthur pursued their protracted long-distance courtship through intermediaries – Kitty's friend, Olivia Sparrow, and an acquaintance of Arthur, Colonel Marcus Beresford.

It took at least four months and often far longer for a letter to reach either Ireland or India. It began when, at Olivia's instigation, Beresford wrote to Arthur in January 1801 enclosing a letter of her own. Beresford wrote that he had come across Kitty at a dinner at Pakenham Hall:

> I don't know what your objects at home may be, but I am certain that you will not take amiss what I say. I know not if Miss Pakenham is an object to you or not – she looks as well as ever – no person whatsoever has paid her any particular attention – so much I say, having heard her name and yours mentioned together. I hear her most highly spoken of by Mrs Sparrow. She lives so retired that nobody ever sees her.[5]

Beresford had artfully passed over Lowry Cole's involvement with Kitty and the fact that the prominent social position of Kitty's brother would have made it all but impossible for Kitty to hide herself away from Dublin society. Through Beresford, Arthur replied to Olivia in August 1801: 'Fortune has favoured me upon every occasion and if I could forget that which has borne so heavily upon me for the last eight years, I should have as little care as you appear to have.' He continued, 'When you see your friend, do me the favour to remember me to her in the kindest manner.'[6]

Writing to Olivia in May 1802, Kitty appeared uncertain of Arthur's true feelings, yet concerned above all for his happiness rather than her own. In view of the wishes of her brother and mother, she knew that 'I can send no message' and 'a kind word from me he might think binding to him and make him think himself obliged to renew a pursuit, which perhaps he might not then wish or my family (at least some of them) take kindly'.[7] She continued,

> My first wish, if I was not taking care not to wish about it, would be that he should return and feel himself perfectly free (I do not mean free from regard for those who sincerely regard him, but to act as he pleases) and then – I hardly know what to wish then, for fear of nursing a disappointment for him, for myself, or a vexation for my friends . . . Perhaps you will be angry with me when I say I am by no means as certain as you seem to be, as to what his present wish is. He now desires to be kindly remembered, but do you not think he seems to think the business over?[8]

Kitty was aware that there were rumours of Arthur's involvement with other officers' wives in India. At least four were said to have been linked with him.[9] Both then and later Kitty seems to have discounted any such gossip, her strong religious beliefs inclining her to pray regularly for forbearance. Kitty suffered ill health and, as the years advanced without Arthur returning, she had become less attractive and less self-confident.

The erratic exchange of correspondence at second hand continued and, as not all letters have survived, it is difficult to judge precisely how Olivia conveyed Kitty's feelings to Arthur. In January 1804 Kitty received a letter Arthur had sent to Olivia in March 1803 in reply to one sent him in May 1802. Arthur had received it in September 1802. He had been so involved in the midst of campaigning against the Marathas that he had not been able to consider it properly. Unsure as to whether either he or Olivia should be more or less discreet regarding Kitty, he again asked to be remembered to her. In turn, Olivia was able to report to Arthur that there had been 'an evident increase in good opinion and interest in those friends who, I have heard, were formerly less favourably inclined towards you and whose heads and hearts can only be influenced by real worth and deserved fame',[10] implying how far his military accomplishments had impressed the Pakenhams.

In a long letter to Olivia in August 1804 Arthur refuted the gossip about his affairs he had heard was circulating at home, hoping that his public services would 'be allowed as a set-off against the faults imputed to a man's private life by scandal and calumny'. He acknowledged that he had not really deserved Kitty's hand when he had first proposed to her, but his love was undimmed: 'Every time that I have heard of her since I left Europe has tended to confirm the impression which had been made on my mind by the former knowledge of, and cannot find words to describe all her good qualities.'[11]

Some years later, Arthur told his confidante, Harriet Arbuthnot, that he felt entrapped, not least by Olivia supposedly sending for him to urge that he renewed his proposal. Arthur had regretted it ever since: 'I was not the least in love with her. I married her because they asked me to do it and I did not know myself. I thought I should never care for anybody again and that I should be with the army and in short I was a fool.'[12]

After so long apart, understandably Kitty and Arthur had perhaps unrealizable expectations of each other. Their worlds had been entirely different and, as a career soldier, Arthur could not be expected to remain at home for any prolonged period of time. Kitty in particular was apprehensive as to her changed appearance – she had put on much weight – and may have feared that her love would not be reciprocated. On Arthur's arrival back in England, Olivia once more acted as go-between. She wrote to Arthur and received the reply that, 'All I can say is that if I could count myself capable of neglecting such a woman, I would endeavour to think of her no more.'[13] Arthur feared that he might be ordered overseas at once, although he had no intention of missing opportunities for further employment. Kitty was fearful of what Arthur intended and confided to Olivia whether she was capable of contributing 'to the comfort or happiness of anybody who has not been in the habit of loving me for years – like my brother or you or mother.'[14]

Arthur wrote formally to Kitty's brother in October 1805, and this time his proposal was accepted. Kitty herself now wrote enquiringly to Arthur,

> It is indeed my earnest wish to see you, besides the pleasure it must give me to meet again an early and truly valued friend, I do not think it fair to engage you before you are quite positively certain that I am indeed the woman you would have for a companion, a friend for life. In so many years I may be much more changed than I am myself conscious of. If when we meet you can tell me with same sincerity which has ever distinguished you through life, that you do not repent having written the letter I am now answering, I shall be most happy.[15]

Kitty was giving him every opportunity of breaking their relationship without losing his honour, but in reply, Arthur proclaimed himself 'the happiest man in the world'. Before proceeding to Ireland, Arthur had spent some days in Cheltenham, where he met the young Vicomtesse de Gontaut-Biron, an exiled French aristocrat. Arthur spoke to her of Kitty and how he had become effectively engaged to a woman who he now wrongly feared had lost her looks through smallpox: 'But she has my promise and my honour demands that I should keep it. It was rather fine of her to write to me with so much simplicity and truth. So I shall start for Ireland at once.'[16]

A suitable financial settlement was rapidly agreed to provide a trust for Kitty and any children in the event of Arthur's death. Arthur's departure for Ireland was delayed by his election as MP for Rye and he arrived in Ireland to see Kitty only on 8 April 1806. The marriage took place in the Longfords' house in Dublin two days later. Arthur then had to return to London to take his seat on 16 April as the Commons was due to vote on the impeachment of his brother, Richard, on 22 April. Richard's handling of the war against the Marathas had been criticised and he had been dismissed as Governor General. There were also allegations of corruption.

Presented at Court in May, Kitty was asked by Queen Charlotte, 'But did you really never write one letter to Sir Arthur Wellesley during his absence?' to which Kitty replied, 'No, never, Madam.' The Queen then asked if Kitty had thought of Arthur: 'Yes, Madam, very often.'[17]

Soon pregnant with a son – Arthur Richard, born in February 1807 – and with Arthur commanding a brigade at Deal, Kitty struggled with the task of managing their new London home in Harley Street. At 35 Kitty was relatively advanced in age for a first pregnancy and it was not without risk. Initially it had taken time to arrange the acquisition of Harley Street and after the wedding Arthur had stayed at his old lodgings and Kitty with a friend. Then Arthur was appointed Chief Secretary for Ireland and he departed for Dublin, although Kitty did join him there in May 1807. When Arthur was appointed to a command in the expedition to Denmark, Kitty stayed in Dublin. Arthur returned in October 1807, but was in London when a second son – Charles – was born in January 1808. In June 1808 Arthur sailed to command the British expeditionary force in Portugal. After a brief campaign, in which Arthur triumphed over the invading French army at Vimeiro but his superiors accepted a disgraceful armistice, he returned once more to Dublin. The death of Sir John Moore at Corunna in January 1809 saw Arthur once more sent to command in the Spanish Peninsula. He was not to see Kitty again for five years.

It was increasingly notable that during Arthur's frequent absences from Harley Street, his surviving letters to Kitty became ever terser. Arthur was consumed with military and political issues and he had no interest in domestic matters, displaying impatience with her enquiries as to household expenses and management. Kitty loaned money to her brother, Henry Pakenham, without telling Arthur, which led to household bills being left unpaid. Arthur only became aware of this later, believing that Kitty had been responsible for considerable deception. He later said he had 'received the impression that he had been grossly deceived, and never afterwards got rid of it'.[18]

He was accustomed to military society and not used to civil or family conversations. She could not adequately discuss military and political matters with his colleagues and was too indiscrete to be trusted with sensitive information. They had little in common which they could discuss. In later years, Arthur's biographer, the Rev. George Gleig, who had known Kitty, recorded that while she was 'very amiable, very religious, entertaining for her husband unbounded admiration, she could not bring herself to take the slightest interest in the subjects which mainly engrossed his attention. Even in the smallest matters their tastes seldom agreed.'[19]

Kitty had been complaining to her mother about Arthur's neglect of her and this seems to have reached him. Kitty was desperate to please Arthur, but was ill-equipped to share in any of the momentous issues confronting him. 'Her preoccupation was with childbirth, his with international affairs.'[20] What added to her gloom was Arthur's absolute direction just before he left for Portugal again that Kitty and his sons must never again set foot in Ireland. It was a reflection primarily of Arthur's impatience with Irish affairs generally as Chief Secretary, but it might also have been a manifestation of his wife's failure to meet the expectations he had invested in her for so many years. Rather than the strong woman he thought he had married, Kitty seemed to him weak and argumentative.

Kitty found little solace in the brief letters she received and resorted to asking the Military Secretary at Horse Guards, Torrens, to keep her secretly informed of Arthur's movements. She sent various comforts for Arthur and he, very occasionally, sent her gifts such as hairbrushes. Her concerns for Arthur's health were clumsily displayed. When, in 1813, she heard Arthur was suffering from rheumatism and lumbago whilst in the Pyrenees, she asked a friend of Arthur and herself, Sir John Malcolm, to obtain some Cazaputta oil she could send out. Yet she told Malcolm that Arthur 'will probably receive my offering with scorn'.[21] Significantly, Arthur had no portrait of her at his headquarters – Kitty did not like sitting for portraits – but did set a watercolour of his two sons in the lid of his dressing case.

Languid is a word that so often appears in the journal Kitty began to keep intermittently in July 1809. A typical entry was 'Ill and Idle. I have nothing to say of this languid day.'[22] Her intention was to record her activities on the left-hand page of the journal and Arthur's on the right. More often than not the right-hand page was blank, as she had so little information to impart, and what there was came from the press. Her entries frequently revealed all too tragically her loneliness. Thus, on 24 July 1809, 'Began the day wretchedly. God forgive me!'[23] On another occasion, she recorded, 'Spent the evening alone and wretchedly! I must try to regain the favour of the Almighty.'[24] In October 1809, with the children ill with whooping cough, she wrote, 'So uninteresting, so unvaried is my life that to keep a daily journal is almost impossible and yet by not doing so I lose the pleasure of knowing how he and I were employed at the same time, which to me is a great pleasure.'[25] One entry in December 1809 simply reads 'Alone and Sad.'[26]

Having moved with the children to Broadstairs for the summer of 1809, Kitty often walked on the pier. The boys especially enjoyed the seaside and at least she was able to glory in their happiness. Kitty took up mending shoes, resumed playing the harp after some years, painted, drew sketches, and read voraciously in the local library, although Arthur later suggested she had not read most of the books she had borrowed.

Evenings were especially difficult. As she noted on one occasion: 'From the time my children go to bed, I find my time torn with the most hateful recollections, but I will not so soon break the resolution I have thought it prudent to form: I will therefore write no more tonight.'[27] Following Arthur's victory at Talavera in July 1809 she regretted that the title he had chosen of Viscount Wellington seemed to signify nothing, not apparently aware that at the suggestion of his elder brother, William Wellesley-Pole, Arthur had chosen it, as Wellington in Somerset was close to the hamlet of Welleslie: William had adopted the Wellesley-Pole surname as a condition for an inheritance, and after Richard's death in 1842 succeeded as Earl of Mornington. Kitty was delighted that her eldest son would now have a title as Baron Douro. Arthur was raised to Earl in February 1812, to Marquis in August 1812, and to Duke in May 1814. He was promoted to Field Marshal in June 1813.

Recording in June 1810 that in the last six months there had not been 'a single day without some degree of pain', she resolved to try to avoid any further indolence.[28] Kitty avoided public functions, which she disliked, not least because she was so ill-informed as to what Arthur was doing, but also because she was short-sighted and much preferred the company of friends. She did dine out frequently and, apart from her own children, also took a hand in bringing up Gerald, the son of Arthur's brother, Henry Wellesley, whose mother had run away with Lord Henry Paget, later Earl of Uxbridge and Marquis of Anglesey.

Over the years Kitty drew great comfort from the love extended to her not just by her two sons, but also by those she effectively and, with a generous heart, adopted. In earlier years she had cared for Arthur's godson, Arthur Freese, Mrs Freese being one of those with whom Arthur had dallied in India. Arthur Freese had been sent home to live with an aunt, but she had died so Kitty took on the task. Many years later, following the death of the Duke of Richmond, his youngest son – another of Arthur's godsons – was to spend holidays with Kitty. Another taken under her wing was her niece, Kate Hamilton.

Yet her deepest pain, that her love of her husband was not returned to her, could not be alleviated and she suffered from bouts of depression. In October 1810 she had apparently sought a degree of reconciliation with her husband, but Arthur's reply was uncompromising. There would be no divorce, but their relationship was 'at an end for ever'.[29] With no apparent thought of the impact of his declaration, Arthur was still sending Kitty instructions to send him provisions and clothing. Kitty recorded in her journal that she spent a 'very wretched night'.[30] The next day her happiness was restored by news of Arthur's victory at Bussaco on 27 September.

Kitty felt further hurt when she read Madame de Staël's novel *Corinne* in March 1811, since it was the story of an English aristocrat abandoning one lover for another.[31] Ironically, Germaine de Staël, although far from attractive in appearance – she was a large, almost masculine-looking woman – was one of those intellectually-gifted and politically-engaged women whose company Arthur enjoyed. He met her in Paris after Napoleon's first abdication and then again after the latter's final defeat. She was a frequent correspondent of Arthur until her death in 1817.

Meanwhile, Kitty was receiving treatment from Dr John Mayo for depression, and she confided to her journal at one point that she had contemplated suicide. She had suffered the tragic death of one of her younger brothers, William, lost at sea in December 1811, which sent her spiralling into the depths of despair, but she was able to surmount her morbid desires and recoiled from the idea of suicide as a solution.

Kitty appears to have recovered her equanimity by the autumn of 1812, although her days were filled much as before. Her sons continued to be her main comfort. She wrote to a friend in November 1812, 'I wish you could see the delight, hear the shouts of joy, with which they fly out of the house after the confinement of a day of rain.'[32] On her wedding anniversary in April 1813, she wrote to her sister,

> My husband is blessed wherever his name is heard. He may possibly soon return to a wife who will no longer worry him because he, soft as well as strong, complying as well as firm, everything that is gentle and domestic: being obliged to live his soldier's hard and wandering life – I am grown wise . . . and rejoice that I have lived to be seven years a wife.[33]

She seemed to believe, even at this stage, that a home life with Arthur was still possible.

Kitty continued to shun the limelight, drawing criticism from Arthur's family for not being seen at the celebrations for his victory at Vitoria in June 1813. Kitty remarked, 'If I did appear, I must be a conspicuous object. My feelings for Lord Wellington's victory cannot, I think, be doubted and surely need not be exhibited . . . Did you ever hear of a really great man whose wife did not like keeping home in the absence of her husband?'[34]

With the first abdication of Napoleon in April 1814, Arthur went at once to Paris as British ambassador to the restored King Louis XVIII.

Surprisingly, he did invite Kitty to join him in Paris. This was a short-lived reunion of sorts, as she arrived in October 1814, but Arthur departed for the Congress of Vienna in February 1815 and Kitty returned home. As always, Kitty had the utmost confidence in Arthur's ability to defeat Napoleon when he returned from exile in Elba once more to challenge the peace of Europe. On the Sunday before Waterloo, she told friends, 'Ah! Wait a little, he is in his element now; depend upon him.'[35]

Following Arthur's final defeat of Napoleon at Waterloo in June 1815, Kitty returned to Arthur's side in Paris in the autumn. She loathed ostentation and found it difficult to dress in the way expected of her. While giving Kitty some credit for her efforts, Lady Elizabeth Yorke commented, 'Her appearance, unfortunately, does not correspond to one's notion of an ambassadress or the wife of a hero . . . '[36] Kitty had attended the opera with Arthur in Paris and had been described in *The Lady's Magazine* as 'shimmering' with humming-birds' feathers. It was not true. Kitty wrote to her childhood friend, the novelist Maria Edgeworth, 'I do not possess any ornaments of feathers – do you recollect on a former occasion your telling me of my having appeared (in the newspapers) blazing with diamonds – my diamonds are yet in the mine & my humming birds yet wear their own feathers.'[37] Kitty once told a friend who asked how many times each day she thought of her dress, 'Why, three times, Morning, evening and night besides *casualties*.'[38]

Aware of the rumours of Arthur's sexual indiscretions in Paris, Maria Edgeworth wrote of Kitty, 'She is not a woman who delights in titles or rank, but she does enjoy her husband's glory and therefore I hope it will not, like Nelson's, be tarnished.'[39] Lady Bessborough felt sorry for Kitty: 'I am afraid he [Arthur] is behaving very ill to that poor little woman; he is found great fault with for it, *not* on account of making her miserable or of the immorality of the fact, but the want of *proceed* and publicity of his attentions to [the Italian singer Guiseppina] Grassini.'[40] Arthur's mood lightened noticeably once Kitty had left Paris, although they had really only met regularly over the dinner table. Nonetheless, it was said that Kitty had made friends with several of Arthur's ADCs and had taken part agreeably in their gossip and party games,[41] something of a change for her.

Arthur's career after Waterloo was meteoric. He represented Britain at the Congress of Aix-la-Chapelle in 1818 and at the Congress of Verona in 1822. He was Master General of the Ordnance with a seat in Cabinet from 1819 to 1827. Following the short-lived government of Lord Goderich, Arthur became Prime Minister in January 1828. However, political issues such as Catholic Emancipation, and especially reform of the House of Commons, dogged Arthur's administration. He continued to lead the Tory Party in opposition after losing the 1830 election to the Whigs, being implacably opposed to the Reform Bill passed in 1832. He was briefly caretaker Prime Minister again for a month in 1834 since Sir Robert Peel was abroad when the Whig government fell. Thereafter he acted as a kind of elder statesman. Commander-in-Chief from 1827 to 1828, Arthur resumed the role in 1842 until his death. He also became Lord Warden of the Cinque Ports in 1839, dying at his official residence of Walmer Castle in Kent on 14 September 1852. By the time of his death, all political controversies had been forgotten and Arthur had become almost a national monument. His funeral two months later on 18 November 1852 was one of the most extraordinary spectacles ever witnessed in Victorian Britain.

During this time, Kitty made her home at Arthur's new country seat of Stratfield Saye, which was presented by a grateful nation in 1817. Their respective suites were at different ends of the house. She devoted herself to bringing up her children, never quite losing her faith in romance. She was now greying and Arthur ungallantly suggested she purchase a wig and apply some rouge to her wan features. He rarely visited Stratfield Saye. Lady Shelley wrote of one party that he did host there, 'The Duchess of Wellington sat apart from her guests, dressed even in winter in white muslin, without any ornaments, when everyone else was in full dress . . . She seldom spoke but looked through her eyeglass lovingly upon the Duke, who sat opposite her.'[42] On another occasion, Arthur found it difficult to amuse one group of guests, as Kitty would not play cards on a Sunday and left him to entertain them.[43] Rather pointedly, Kitty would refer to those brought to Stratfield Saye by Arthur as the 'Duke's company'.

Arthur was aggrieved that Kitty and her family were complaining about his conduct towards her, and there is no doubt that some of Kitty's friends were making things worse. Maria Edgeworth thought that Kitty 'has been more hurt by her friends than her enemies, and more by herself than by both put together – but still, if she does not quite wash out his affections with tears, they will be hers during the long autumn of life'.[44] Arthur was hardly free of blame in so obviously neglecting her for other women. So widespread was the belief that Arthur was treating Kitty badly, that one of those involved in the abortive Cato Street Conspiracy to murder the entire Cabinet in February 1820 claimed this justified killing Arthur.[45] Arthur believed the rumours had been started by Kitty and her family. He accused them of 'watching & spying' on him, and that servants had been asked to do so.[46] Arthur wrote angrily to Kitty in April 1820 that 'every day's experience convinces me that you do more foolish things . . . which you must regret . . . upon the first moment of reflection than any woman in the world'.[47]

In May 1821 Arthur received a letter from Kitty with a list of those to whom he had not offered charity. He interpreted it as unwarranted criticism, and again accused Kitty of using the servants to spy on him. He threatened, 'If it goes on I must live somewhere else. It is the meanest dirtiest trick of which anybody can be guilty.' Kitty responded by asking for a list of those charities he wished to support so that she would not pay out twice to those making claims on her at Stratfield Saye. She felt herself 'incapable of any mean or dirty action as you are yourself' and hoped 'that I may not again be subjected to offensive accusations for which there is [*sic*] positively no grounds whatever'.[48] A further letter from Kitty crossed with one from Arthur, again complaining about the request for lists of his favoured charities and returning to the charge of spying: 'If you are to continue to ask & obtain information of what I do from any servant or dependant of mine or anybody else excepting myself, I'll not live in the same House with you.'[49]

Kitty, believing herself to be dying, on 9 July 1821 sent an accusatory 'last' letter forgiving him:

> I would I am sure, could have made you happy had you suffered me
> to try, but thrust from you I was not allowed, for God's sake for your

own dear sake for Christ sake do not use another woman as you have
treated me, never write to a human being such letters as those from
you which I now enclose; they have destroyed me.[50]

In 1822 Arthur refused to increase Kitty's allowance from £500 to £670
per annum, discovering that she was giving away half to various charitable
endeavours. Kitty confessed, 'I believe I may have given away money very
injudiciously, perhaps sometimes to spare myself the pain of refusing, and
I confess it would be hard to make you pay for my weakness. I will from
this time only retain as permanent pensioners those who are so very old
& friends that they must perish without my assistance.'[51] Her 'pensioners'
included a retired miniature painter who had once taught her, a disabled
dancing master, her sons' former wet-nurse, an old maid and an old servant
with a crippled child.

Arthur had always found Kitty dull and simple-minded, the latter a
judgement also levelled against her by Arthur's former ADC Lord William
Lennox.[52] Lady Shelley again recorded on one occasion that Kitty had all
the faults Arthur most despised, 'lack of common sense, ignorance of the
world, obstinacy about trifles, Calvinistic and strong religious feelings'.[53]
Lady Shelley also suggested that Kitty was spoiling her sons, writing
she was 'a slave of the boys when they came home for the holidays [from
Eton]. I have seen her carrying their fishing-nets, their bats, balls and
stumps, apparently not perceiving how bad it was for them to regard a
woman, far less their mother, as a simple drudge, fit only to minister to
their pleasure.'[54] Worse from Arthur's point of view, he thought Kitty had
invested her sons with a wariness towards him, which irritated him greatly.
Harriet Arbuthnot doubted this, writing in July 1826, 'he is unjust, for the
D[uche]ss wd do anything she possibly could to put him & his children
well together if she knew how, but she is such a fool that she does not'.[55]
Later, Arthur said neither he nor his brother had ever been shown the least
affection by their father.[56] At least on one occasion, however, when Arthur
was home from Paris in July 1816, Kitty was delighted to find Arthur had
time for the boys, 'I say with delight they are as fond of and as familiar
with their noble and beloved Father as if they had never been separated
from him. They accompany him on his walks, *chat* with him, play with

him. In short they are the chosen companions of each other . . .'[57] It was as they grew older that Arthur had less interest in them.

Kitty continued to run up debts, Arthur paying off £10,000 at her death and then discovering another £10,000-worth, much having been given away to Kitty's relatives. The newly discovered debts included a £2,000 bond taken out in 1822, and of which Arthur had been unaware, which had likely gone to Kitty's sister's family whose bank had failed. Wearily Arthur wrote that this had 'revived the recollection of many transactions which I had wished and determined to bury in oblivion'. He felt that debts had always preyed on Kitty's mind.[58] Not long after Kitty's death, Arthur told Lady Salisbury that Kitty had been 'a sort of wise and uneducated folly, an obliquity in all her view of things, which it was impossible to remove'.[59]

Arthur, meanwhile, had pursued other women in abundance. The memoirs of the courtesan Harriette Wilson are not be relied upon, but there is little doubt that Arthur was introduced to her on his return from India. Famously, he refused to pay up for the omission of his name from her memoirs, published in 1825, with the apocryphal, 'Publish and be damned'. Salacious gossip, however, did not materially affect Arthur's career. Arthur was supposed to have kept Lady Conyngham as a mistress at his headquarters in Portugal in 1809. It was said that after Arthur's triumphal entrance into Madrid in August 1812, 'Lady Wellington would be jealous if she were to hear of his proceedings. I never saw him in his carriage without two or three ladies.'[60] Among many Portuguese and Spanish women who flocked around Arthur and his officers, at least one was said to have accompanied him as his mistress on the final advance into France in October 1813.[61] In Paris before Kitty arrived to join Arthur, he had been surrounded by numerous attractive and admiring women and certainly had affairs with two of Napoleon's old mistresses, the Italian singer Guiseppina Grassini and the actress Marguerite Weimer, known as Mademoiselle Georges.

Arthur generally enjoyed the company of attractive and confident women, although this did not necessarily imply more than flirting. He was soon being accompanied by Lady Georgiana Lennox, Lady Charlotte Greville and Lady Frances Wedderburn-Webster. Arthur wrote to all three during the ensuing Waterloo campaign. It was alleged that the reason Arthur had been late for the celebrated Duchess of Richmond's ball on 15 June, the eve of the Battle of Quatre Bras, was that he was with Lady Frances, although she was actually heavily pregnant at the time. The rumours resulted in Lady Frances's husband, Captain James Wedderburn-Webster, winning a libel case against the proprietors of the *St James Chronicle* in 1816 after Arthur had convinced the husband that there were no grounds for him to take divorce proceedings against his wife. It appeared that the captain's mother-in-law, Lady Mountnorris, had been responsible for some of the rumours. There were many others who flirted with Arthur, including Frances, Lady Shelley, and some who became mistresses such as Marianne Paterson, the young wife of an American businessman. She subsequently married Richard Wellesley, to Arthur's evident disgust. Arthur had the capacity to fall for several beauties at once and his dalliances continued to the end of his life. In 1847, and quite unconventionally, the philanthropic heiress Angela Burdett-Coutts, even proposed to Arthur but he declined on the grounds of the age difference – he was now 77 and she only 32.

It was to this continuing background that Kitty had to resign herself. It is difficult to judge how seriously Arthur took his many admirers in romantic terms although he certainly kept up a correspondence with several of them. Most prominent of all, however, was his relationship with Harriet Arbuthnot. She and Arthur certainly loved each other. Speculation abounded, extending to Sir Robert Peel and Charles Greville and to Kitty, but Harriet does not appear to have been Arthur's mistress. Her religious convictions and her own keen sense of moral propriety almost certainly precluded it. More importantly, she played a much more significant role in his life than any other woman and most certainly more so than Kitty. Her early death was clearly a considerable blow to Arthur.

Arthur met Harriet in 1814. She was 21 and had married Charles Arbuthnot, a 46-year-old widower with four sons earlier that year. Arbuthnot was well connected politically as a long-serving Joint Secretary to the Treasury from 1809 to 1823. Thus, Harriet, whose father was the second son of the Earl of Westmorland, moved in the highest social and political circles and did so with ease. Politically astute, it was Harriet rather than Kitty who presided over the political dinners Arthur hosted at his new London residence of Apsley House, purchased from Richard in 1817. Her influence was such that she played a key role in discussing its extension with the architect Benjamin Wyatt and policing Wyatt's bills.[62] In contrast to Kitty, Harriet was able to indulge in the kind of informed conversation that Arthur welcomed. Arthur wrote an estimated 1,500 letters to her between 1818 and her death in 1834. Harriet shared Arthur's politics and she revelled in his company: 'It is quite refreshing to be in constant and habitual intercourse with a mind so enlightened and so superior as his is, which is familiar with every subject and whom at the same time, can find amusement in the most ordinary occupations of life.'[63] Such sentiments would have been entirely beyond poor Kitty.

Although they did not always agree, Harriet had more influence than any other woman in Arthur's life. He took her views seriously. Her friendship with him was greatly resented by those who aspired to such a role such as Sarah, Lady Jersey, Emily, Lady Cowper, Lady Granville and Countess (later Princess) Lieven, wife of the Russian ambassador in London. Harriet's journals show her counselling Arthur over such issues as his relationship with the King, Irish affairs and Catholic Emancipation. She had strong views on Tory politicians whom she disliked, such as Peel and Canning. She told him plainly that he should not have accepted Goderich's offer of becoming Commander-in-Chief in January 1827 when he did not support Goderich's government.[64] Arthur was angry, but their friendship was undimmed. She also thought he should resign as Prime Minister as early as 1829. Harriet was never afraid of confronting Arthur. Lady Shelley recorded that Harriet 'gave him her clear and honest opinion on matters of which others were afraid to speak'.[65] As Harriet herself wrote on one occasion in November 1828,

> He said I told him always the most disagreeable things in the most invidious manner and that he would take care never to tell me anything again or ask my opinion – and I, on the other hand, got at last into a passion, too, assured him I would never tell him the truth again and

that if that was his way of behaving, he would neither deserve a friend nor have one. [66]

A shouting match ensued on the Mall, but it ended 'as we always do' with the two making up, for Arthur 'never likes one a bit the less for telling him unpleasant truths'. By contrast, Kitty concealed much from Arthur, not least her financial mismanagements. In 1825 Lady Shelley noted, 'The words "Don't tell your Father" were ever on her lips – she even tried to induce her visitors to share in this folly. She often said to me "Don't tell the Duke – now mind don't tell the Duke".'[67]

Arthur frequently discussed his 'domestic annoyances' with Harriet. He told Harriet that, despite his efforts to live with Kitty amicably, she did not understand him, was obstinate and 'never for one instant supposes that when our opinions differ, she may be the one in the wrong'. Kitty also made his house 'so dull that nobody would go to it' and 'it drove him to seek abroad that comfort & happiness that was denied to him at home'.[68] Arthur also complained that those whom Kitty did invite to Stratfield Saye were almost entirely unknown to him: 'The Duchess has certainly the most extraordinary fancy in the selection of her acquaintances.'[69]

Harriet thought Kitty,

> certainly the silliest woman I have ever met with, & I must own that I think she now does not appear to have the slightest desire to please him. She does not comply with any of his fancies in the arrangement of his house, & in truth it is so bad a *ménage* it is quite disagreeable to be in the house.[70]

Harriet continued that Kitty dressed like a housekeeper or a shepherdess rather than a lady. On another occasion, she wrote that Kitty,

> is the most abominably silly, stupid woman that ever was born; but I told the Duke I thought he was to blame, too, for that all would go much better if he would be civil to her, but he is not. He never speaks to her and carefully avoids ever going near her . . . Poor woman! I am sorry for her; she cannot help being a fool, & never was a person so mismatched. I am sorry for him too. It drives him from his home & he is getting tired of running about the world.[71]

Kitty's health began to deteriorate in 1829: she may have developed stomach cancer. She was much agitated by the duel fought between Arthur and the Earl of Winchelsea on 23 March 1829, the Earl being stoutly opposed to Arthur's policy of granting Catholic Emancipation. In the event, Arthur fired deliberately wide and the Earl fired in the air. Kitty was so agitated that she could only write to Arthur Richard five days later. On the other hand, she was greatly relieved when Arthur resigned as Prime Minister in November 1830.

There was a degree of reconciliation at that time, as Kitty agreed to take a role as joint guardian to the three children of Arthur's dissolute nephew, William Wellesley-Pole. She moved up to Apsley House in the spring of 1830, but could no longer manage to climb the stairs, so a suite was prepared for her on the ground floor. Kitty suffered two bad falls and became increasingly bedridden. For the first time Kitty discovered that Arthur wore an amulet she had given to him many years previously. He remarked, 'She found it as she would have found it any time these twenty years had she cared to look for it.'[72] He also found it 'a strange thing that two people can live together for half a lifetime and only understand one another at the very end'.[73]

At the end of Kitty's life, Arthur spent long periods at her bedside, showing a patience and softness that had not previously marked his attitude towards her. Kitty died on 24 April 1831, Arthur holding her hand and her eldest son beside her. Perhaps he finally felt remorse; perhaps it was a memory of much earlier times, but he had never before treated her with sensitivity or kindness. Kitty's love and devotion had never wavered. When Maria Edgeworth was visiting her and glanced at some of the mementos of Arthur's victories in the room, Kitty weakly lifted herself in her bed and said, 'All tributes to merit! There's the value; all pure, no corruption ever suspected even. Even of the Duke of Marlborough that could not be said so truly.' Maria sadly wrote, 'There she lies fading away, still feeding, when she can feed on nothing else, on his glories, on the perfume of his incense.'[74] Maria hoped that Kitty 'will not outlive the pleasure she now feels, I am assured in the Duke's returning kindness and 'not last too long and tire out that easily tired pity of his'.[75] Just before her death Kitty wrote to a friend saying an old French song had been on her mind, 'For my folly is to love him. I will love him all my life.'[76] Lady Wharncliffe recorded,

> So the poor little Duchess of Wellington is gone at last! I am told she suffer'd but little, & was latterly so happy at the Duke's kindness & attention to her, that she said she never knew what happiness was before. Poor little soul, how well for her that she *did* die then! I am glad for his own sake, as well as hers, that he did his duty by her at last. I hear he sat up with her the last night.[77]

Kitty's miserable marriage to the Iron Duke was bookended by two periods of happiness. During their initial courtship of ten years when, by proxy, letters declaring their love for each other, Kitty yearned for the happiness that never materialized. Then, sadly, during her final months of sickness, when Arthur was tender towards her, and her unrequited love was in some measure returned. In the intervening years, Kitty bore the burden of lost love, replaced by his dislike of, and irritation towards her, with great fortitude. However, his initial love for her undoubtedly spurred him on to become one of Britain's greatest generals.

Chapter 3

Campaign Child Bride: Juana Smith

A firework display fit for a king tore through the skies of Badajoz during the night hours of 6 April 1812. The 22-day siege of the city by Wellington's army was drawing to a close. Citizens cowered, not in fear of the pyrotechnics, but of the carnage that would follow. The tradition of centuries was that if a fortress would not yield, the defenders could expect no mercy if the assault was successful. The aftermath of this siege was no exception. The victors claimed their barbaric right to plunder homes and ravish women; the town was sacked and many inhabitants killed, with no exception for gender or age. Amidst desperate screams, two young women of the old Spanish aristocracy, the orphaned 14-year-old Juana Maria de los Dolores de Leon and her older married sister ran through smouldering streets, running the gauntlet of grasping hands and lustful mouths in fear for their lives.

Outside the walls were a group of officers less inclined to partake in the murderous exploits of their comrades-in-arms. Two young officers stood away from the city wall and beckoned the two women to safety. The decision to trust this offer of sanctuary was a difficult one for the older sister. Her instinct probably told her to keep running, but 'so great, she said, was her confidence in our national character that she knew the appeal would not be made in vain, nor the confidence abused'.[1] Something in the bearing of the two officers led her to a decision which was to change the life of her younger sister beyond anything either of them could ever have imagined.

Captain Harry Smith of the 95th Rifles recalled, 'But yesterday she and her younger sister were able to live in affluence – today they knew not where to lay their heads, nor get a morsel of bread.' Blood was trickling down their necks, caused by 'the wrenching of earrings through flesh by the hands of those, worse than savages, who would not take the trouble to unclasp them'.[2] Harry referred to the post-victory carnage at Badajoz as 'a scene of horror I would willingly forget', adding that 'Civilised man when let loose and the bonds of morality relaxed, is a far greater beast than the savage, more refined in his cruelty, more fiend-like in every act.' He was able to reflect that the terrible acts were the catalyst for 'the solace and the whole happiness of my life, when a poor defenceless maiden of thirteen years was thrown upon my generous nature'.[3] Two weeks later, this young girl, Juana, was to become his wife.

Juana is believed to have been a direct descendant of Ponce de Leon, Knight of Romance, who went to Florida in search of the legendary fountain of youth. Hers was one of the oldest Spanish, but not Moorish, families. In better days the family had entertained high-ranking officers and British nobility. Their prosperity from abundant olive groves was ended by the destruction of their crops by the 'unsparing hand of the French'.[4] Juana had already survived two previous sieges of Badajoz; in one she had cradled her mortally-wounded brother as he died in her arms. This high-born young Spanish girl, raised in a suffocatingly strict convent, gave up her family, friends, country and, most significantly, her Catholic faith to marry Harry Smith. Had any member of her family, apart from her sister, who was in no position to offer home or shelter, been present after the 1812 siege, the marriage would certainly not have been allowed to take place. Similarly it would have been deemed immensely damaging to Harry's career had he converted to Catholicism, and it is not likely that the religious difficulty would have been overlooked. Even at 14 years of age Juana well knew the implications of what she was about to do. It was not until the early 1830s, whilst living in Cape Town, that Juana formally became a member of the Church of England, but to all intents and purposes she had abandoned any links with the Catholic Church from the day she wed Harry. The implications of such an action according to the Catholic Church at the time included excommunication and a list of penances, taking in eternal damnation. Juana understood this, but was not deterred from grasping the chance of happiness and security with one who must have seemed a knight in shining armour.

Harry Smith's companion outside the city wall, Johnny Kincaid, also of the 95th, was said to remark of Juana that 'she was so beautiful that to look at her was to love her',[5] although he never told her. In his memoirs, Kincaid describes her countenance as 'more English than Spanish . . . her face, though not perhaps rigidly beautiful, was irresistibly attractive, surmounting a figure cast in nature's fairest mould'.[6] He correctly predicted that 'from the moment she was thrown on her own resources, her star was in the ascendant'.[7]

Harry Smith, born in 1787 in Whittlesey, Cambridgeshire, was one of eleven children and said that 'Every pain was taken with my education which my father could afford'.[8] Harry's father was a surgeon, an honourable and well-paid profession. To his family and peers, the idea of the 24-year-old Harry marrying a mere child seemed ridiculous. At the time of his marriage his fellow officers were sure that it would stunt the progress of his rapidly-rising military career and that he would neglect his duty. 'Alas', they concluded, 'poor Harry Smith is lost, who was the example of a duty officer previously. It is only natural he must neglect his duty now.' Harry's response was that having to provide for a wife would only serve to motivate him more: 'My love will excite me to exertions in the hope of preferment.'[9] He also remarked that his wife 'had the sense to understand that his duty was all important',[10] a statement that was as true of Juana at 14 as it was on Harry's dying day.

From the outset, Juana was eager to improve her considerable accomplishments, particularly in horsemanship and Harry was enthusiastic to assist. 'My wife could not ride in the least at first, although she had frequently ridden on a donkey,' he remarked. She soon wanted her own horse. 'When you can ride as well as you can dance and sing, you shall,' Harry promised.[11] Juana improved so rapidly that she was soon an accomplished horsewoman and surprised many with her competence in controlling beasts more suited to stronger, robust males.

It was observed that she never complained when he was gone, and that her first question to Harry on upon his return from a day in combat or marching was always 'Are you sure you have done your duty?'[12] Harry admitted that, duty done, he abandoned himself to the charms of his young wife. Wherever Harry was posted, Juana never expressed dismay at the prospect of a difficult climate or journey and the effect it might have on their health. The important factor for her was only that she could be with him. It is fair to assume that she would rather have been with him to nurse him through any sickness, and even to die with him, than to be apart. Harry served through the remainder of the Peninsular War and was then ordered in May 1814 to embark direct from the captured city of Bordeaux to join the staff of the British army in North America: the 'War of 1812' between Britain and the United States had broken out in June 1812. Harry was back home in March 1814. Juana then accompanied him to join Wellington's army in Belgium.

Prior to the final confrontation between Napoleon and Wellington at Waterloo in June 1815, Juana pleaded with Harry that she not be sent away from the battle. More often than not, she was able to persuade Harry to comply with her wishes, but on this occasion Juana was forced to follow his wish for her to return to safety with the command 'That is an order,'[13] in much the same way as he would have addressed his men. She knew better than to resist.

Previously, before the Battle of Nivelle in November 1813, Juana confided in Harry her premonition that 'You or your horse will be killed tomorrow.' Harry brushed off her remark, saying 'Well, of two such chances, I hope it may be the horse.'[14] Juana's prophesy was proved true, when Harry's horse was shot and may even have saved Harry's life by shielding him from enemy fire as he jumped off. He recalled, 'she fell upon me with a crash, which I thought had squeezed me as flat as a thread paper, her blood, like a fountain, pouring into my face'.[15] The sight of Harry on his return, bloody from head to toe, caused Juana to believe that he was so seriously wounded that he was about to die. He reassured her that the blood was not his but that of the horse, who had perished that day.

The Smiths' marriage, though childless, was happy and long-lasting. It is believed that in January 1816, at Cambrai, where Harry was now serving with the Army of Occupation, Juana had been seriously ill, apparently the result of a miscarriage, and for three days it was thought she might not live. Harry's fear for her safety put him in a constant state of terror; at no stage of their marriage did either party thrive when separated. Following their time in France, Harry and Juana had a year in Jamaica, before Harry – now a lieutenant colonel – was posted to the Cape as Deputy Quartermaster General in 1829. They were to remain in South Africa until early 1840. He was then sent to command the British forces confronting the hostile Xhosa tribes on the Eastern Cape frontier in January 1835, at the outbreak of the Sixth Cape Frontier (Kaffir) War. Harry was widely regarded as having saved the frontier in British Kaffraria.

Impatient and uxorious, having been parted from Juana for four months, Harry felt it had been much longer, exclaiming 'four months . . . Good Heavens! Four years at least.'[16] His dislike of being apart from his 'old wife' or 'old woman' as he continually referred to Juana, even while she was still young, was a constant theme in his many letters to her and others over the years. Even during short separations, Harry consistently wrote to Juana, even though he may have been dictating official letters until after midnight, he always hand-wrote the ones to Juana. His letters contain many accounts of what was happening on his campaigns and battlefields, an indication of his belief in her as an intellectual equal. He wrote to her of Somerset as a 'contemptible wretch as much afraid of me as of responsibility. His conduct has been puny, more like a schoolboy than a man of any sort of energy.'[17] At one point, in language that may have been perceived as offensive, even in Harry's day, he wrote to Juana 'I have gained credit for two things: licking the Kaffirs; another, blowing up the lazy rascals who will neither work, fight nor do anything other than draw rations.'[18] He used his letters to Juana as a means of relating things nearer the truth than he was prepared to admit to anyone else. His letters tell of his true feelings towards some of the country peoples he encountered. Of Maqoma, a Xhosa chief, he wrote 'he is a very sensible, shrewd fellow with a heart, and, for a savage, wonderfully clever'.[19]

He also wrote of more trivial matters, telling her one occasion that 'there were forty people in my room, while I am lying on my bed full of tea'.[20] He wrote when learning that she was in pain due to rheumatism that he 'wished he were there to massage her beautiful legs'.[21] Given the privation and hardship that Juana suffered between periods of luxury, it is hardly surprising that she was afflicted in this way, and Harry's touching note reminds us of the closeness of their relationship. Harry did, however, pay attention to attractive women and Juana was aware of this. She enquired about the women in Grahamstown, and Harry replied 'You are in no danger, alma mia, of being supplanted. This is the most dull, stupid and horrid place on earth, celebrated for the most ugly of the fair sex.'[22] We can assume from the light-heartedness of his reply that Harry was a faithful husband and that Juana trusted him. They shared a sense of humour, apparent in many of Harry's letters, 'I have just had a nice bit of wood put on the fire,' he writes. 'Oh that you were sitting with me – whereas that ugly beast Balfour [his ADC] is warming his behind at it.'[23] Harry was enchanted by the beauty of the land around him, and wrote to Juana of his intent to own a large swathe of it. Despite the fact that Juana was 37 and they had been married and childless for twenty-three years, Harry wrote of the land, 'It may do for our children, but I shall never live on it with my dear old woman.'[24] It is hard to imagine how Juana may have felt upon receiving such a letter. Possibly a deep sadness, but it was not a topic upon which she let her feelings be known.

Harry declared that the only holidays he felt he had were when he was able to lose himself in writing to Juana. She encouraged him, telling him that his letters were her 'only food'.[25] Harry's greatest wish, which he confided in Juana by letter was that, 'please Almighty God, I shall have this old woman with me until we both dwindle to our mother earth, and when the awful time comes, grant we go together at the same moment'.[26]

His devotion to her was so great that Harry admitted that when alone at home he would take one of her gowns out her cupboard and 'am fool enough to kiss it and fold it in my arms'. He was so lonely on campaign at Inkosi, he wrote beseeching Juana to join him. 'Once more we will go everywhere together,' he wrote. 'As the old man campaigns so well, why should not the old woman?'[27] In response to his request, Juana embarked upon a treacherous 600-mile journey, which necessitated travelling in a covered wagon on uneven roads, through mountain passes and across fast-flowing rivers. She averaged about 70 miles a day.

During difficult and dangerous wars, he often wrote in complete contrast to the difficulties he was encountering, of the boredom and tedium he found overwhelming. He felt that no-one other than his dearest wife could understand him and would not judge him. Juana embraced all aspects of the military life to the extent that at times their household 'resembled a military depot – tents, blankets, canteens, boots and so forth lay all about'.[28] Many wives may not have been so tolerant of the inconveniences this caused in their day-to-day lives, especially when still called upon to entertain in the formal way required of them.

Throughout his career, Harry was always slow to believe that he was in any way unpopular with those in his command or those above him. In a letter to Juana, during the Sixth Cape Frontier War, he mentions a group of Dutchmen who had come to his tent to bid him goodbye in May 1835: 'They all march tomorrow thank Heaven. I do pity them: but if ever Job had to deal with them, I feel satisfied he would not have acquired his character for patience.' Following his above remarks he added, 'I am liked by them however, notwithstanding the many rowings I have given them.'[29] To her eternal credit, Juana never enlightened him to the truth that at times her husband was the object of derision and animosity. Her devotion to him never faltered, though she was well aware of her husband's frequent lack of objectivity and tendency to view situations as he would like them to be, rather than what they truly were.

He also tended to take a self-congratulatory view of the role he played in various positive outcomes, such as the securing of peace with the Xhosa in September 1835. The Colonial Secretary, Lord Glenelg, rejected Harry's proposals to annexe what was known as Queen Adelaide Territory. Glenelg's disapproval of Harry prevented him from gaining promised promotion and a posting to India. When Glenelg left the Colonial Office, however, Harry was promoted full colonel and appointed Adjutant General in India. Harry distinguished himself in the short-lived Gwalior campaign, and gained his knighthood as a result of his services at the Battle of Maharajpore in December 1843. Given command of a division during the First Sikh War of 1845–6, Harry again distinguished himself at the Battle of Aliwal on 28 January 1846, much praise being extended to the 'Hero of Aliwal' including a baronetcy.

A further reward was the appointment of the now Major General Sir Harry Smith, Bt. to the Cape as Governor, Harry and Juana arriving back in South Africa in December 1847. It was to test Harry to the limit. Harry's vision was to bring more white settlers to Kaffraria and integrate the Xhosa through exposure to the extension of missionary-led education and imparting agricultural improvement. But Harry's handling of the government's frustrated desire to send convicts to the Cape in 1849 did not please the Colonial Office. In 1852 Harry was dismissed, the government taking the view that the continuing lack of military success required new leadership. Harry turned down command of the Madras Army as he believed his own health and that of Juana would suffer too much, and saw out his career in the Western and Northern Districts in Britain, retiring in September 1859.

Many times during their marriage, Juana was the stronger psychologically, and those who knew the couple well were aware of this, and were not averse to treating Juana as a trustworthy and capable pair of hands to undertake duties that, by rights, should have been shouldered by Harry. He was so overcome by emotion prior to their departure from Cape Town in April 1852 that he was unable to receive visitors wishing him well and declined to attend a public function held in his honour. It fell to Juana and the aide–de–camp to uphold these social duties with dignity and good grace. Harry was so completely devoid of energy and spirit that it was left to Juana to hold a 'forced sale' of their considerable property, including horses and carriages, and she left Westbrook and Government House to the new governor.[30] Those organizing the events surrounding the Smiths' departure wished to present him with a commemorative plate and a signed document from 'the merchants and other inhabitants'. Juana accepted it, due to her husband's indisposition. Smith's nephew, Colonel Garvock, acting as his private secretary, handed the deputation a written reply on behalf of Smith, stating that Smith regarded the years he had spent as the Cape as being among the happiest of his life, adding the significant caveat, except those during which he had been governor.[31] The cloud over their departure being the result of a less than glittering term of office, was difficult to endure.

All these events must surely have been as painful for Juana as for her husband, but she proved herself superior in stamina, both physically and mentally. It may well have come as no surprise to those around them that it would be Juana who could be relied upon to take the lead and perform the duties that Harry was unable to face. Juana kept her grief to herself until the final emotional procession to the quayside. At this point the horses were removed from the carriage and it was drawn down Adderley Street by members of the excited crowd. Smith was reported to have responded as cheerfully as he could, while his wife wept.[32] It was as if Juana had kept herself able to perform the more formal duties, but was unprepared for the sight of those she had come to know and love pulling their carriage the final few yards of their journey away from a place that had seen some of the happiest times of their lives.

Over the years, Juana found the continuing uncertainty of Harry's safety the hardest thing to bear during all the campaigns. Juana, normally so indomitable, was deeply apprehensive when a battle was in progress. Paradoxically it was more unnerving to be in the rear of the army than at the front. As Lehmann suggested, 'There was generally a scene of uproar and panic among the confused non-combatants.'[33] Her determination and courage in the face of what she believed to be Harry's certain death, spurred her into risking her own life and exhibiting a strength of character many would never attain.

In the campaign of 1813 in the Peninsula, during an attack, Juana was watching the fighting from the window of the cottage they were occupying, 'barely without range of musketry'. She noticed a horse dragging the body of its rider by the stirrup, over rough and stony ground. Believing it to be Harry, 'with one shriek she rushed towards it', completely overtaken by her desire to help her husband, with no concern for her own safety. In the event the rider being dragged along was not Harry, and when she discovered this she is reported as having 'fell senseless from emotion'.[34] True to form, Juana soon recovered.

On the afternoon of 18 June 1815, news reached Juana that the British had won the Battle of Waterloo. She ordered her horse to be made ready at 3am in order for her to join her husband, 'whatever shape fate had reduced him to'.[35] By 7am Juana and her escort, West, arrived in Brussels. On enquiring of her husband she was told that he had been killed. She wrote, 'The road was nearly choked which was to lead me to the completion of my life; to die on the body of the only thing on earth to love, and which I loved with a faithfulness which few can or ever did feel, and none ever exceeded.'[36] Had she discovered his body, there is little doubt that this young girl of 17 would gladly have taken her own life. She galloped past newly-dug graves, in dread of her worst fear that 'he has been buried and I shall never again behold him'. After several agonising examinations of bodies along the corpse strewn road, and none were his, Juana appealed to God, through Jesus Christ, as she had been taught during her convent years. She reported later,

> A guardian angel, a dear and mutual friend, Charlie Gore, appeared to me. In my agony and hope, I exclaimed 'Oh, where is he? Where is my Henrique?'
>
> 'Why near Bavay by this time, as well as ever he was in his life; not wounded even.'
>
> 'The soldiers tell me Brigade- Major Smith is killed.'
>
> 'Dearest Juana, believe me it is poor Charlie Smyth. I left Harry riding Lochinvar in perfect health.'
>
> 'Then God has heard my prayer.'[37]

Juana recalled that the 'sudden transition from my depth of grief and maddening despair was enough to turn my brain, but Almighty God sustained me'.[38]

In April 1814 came the first time that it had not been possible for Juana, to accompany Harry on tour. He was posted to serve in the war in America. Harry had so far failed to gain the promotion he had hoped for, and this posting was seen as an opportunity for advancement. Harry dreaded having to impart this news to Juana. With her customary bravery,

Juana agreed that it was the right thing to do, stating 'and neither of us must repine'. Withholding her true feelings, she added of her forthcoming stay in England with Harry's family, 'I must be expatriated . . . go among strangers, while I lose the only thing on earth my life hangs on and clings to.'[39] At their time of separation, not daring to look back lest he should change his mind, he later remarked, 'God only knows the number of staggering and appalling dangers I had faced, but thank the Almighty, I was never unmanned until now, and I leaped on my horse by that impulse which guides the soldier to do his duty.'[40]

Harry's brother Tom accompanied Juana to England. In sharp contrast to her life in Badajoz, the crowds and traffic of the London streets proved difficult to adjust to. Tom entreated her to stay with the family, but Juana felt acutely aware of her lack of mastery of the English language, and resolved that before meeting Harry's family for the first time, she would take English lessons. She may have hoped that this would raise her status in the eyes of the family of the one she so dearly loved. In no way did she wish to present herself to them as a needy, sorrowful foreign shackle of a bride, but was determined that they should take the view of those who knew her well as an asset to her husband in all situations.

Juana's first tutor was a prim spinster more accustomed to teaching young ladies of high-born families. She was shocked and horrified by some of the less-than-ladylike phrases that Juana had picked up from Riflemen during the campaigns. It was not that Juana meant to offend her tutor; she had no real idea of how inappropriate some of the phrases might be to a lady of little experience beyond the polite drawing room and its niceties. The lady felt unable to continue with her pupil, and was replaced by a more broadminded elderly gentleman, who was able to see the humour in the situation, and coached her in language, phrases and pronunciation more fitting for her prospective meeting with her new family.

Upon his return from America in December, four months after their parting, Juana spotted Harry's hand on the window of the coach that carried him to her London address, crying out 'Oh, Dios, la mano de mi Henrique!'[41] Years later Harry recalled the experience that they had shared on their reunion. He believed it had qualities that were familiar to very few and said, 'Oh you who enter into holy wedlock for the sake of connexions – tame, cool, amiable, good, I admit – you cannot feel what we did. That moment of our lives was worth the whole of your apathetic ones for years.'[42] Despite her unhappiness during their separation, Juana's ambition for her husband's career path was equal to his; she viewed his subsequent promotion to major as 'The reward of our separation'.[43]

Harry's impulsive marriage to Juana had certainly not been for connections. It would have been impossible to predict at that time what amazing qualities and positive influences that Juana would bring to a partnership originally forged as a rescue package for a helpless and distressed young girl of just 14. With her newly-acquired better command of Harry's native tongue, and the possession of qualities similar to those imparted by a finishing school, Juana was newly confident in being able to communicate in a way that might dispel his family's expectation of a haughty, precocious, Spanish child bride. This did not, however, prevent them from playing a trick on Harry's father who was to meet them in London prior to accompanying them to Whittlesey, the family home. While Juana was preparing herself for the meeting, Harry told his father that Juana was 'of the stiff Spanish School as stately as a swan and about as proud as a peacock'. Juana liked the fun of deception, and made her entry in full Spanish costume and swept into the room with a haughty posture. She was unable to maintain this pose, and 'casting aside all restraint, she threw herself into his father's arms, who cried like a child'.[44]

Despite her own reservations, Juana possessed the ability to charm everyone she met. This was not a contrived effort on her part, but a natural quality, which worked its magic with royalty and those in command, to the lowliest of soldiers and those from poor communities. Harry's family were no exception, and she was welcomed with an 'outpouring of love and affection',[45] and soon became one of their own. Juana may have felt a new security and sense of belonging, having lost all contact with her own family, and she was better able to bear the ensuing separation when Harry was recalled to America in December 1814.

The years that followed would prove that Harry Smith had indeed married well. Harry expressed his longstanding devotion to Juana in part of a speech in June 1847 at a ball at Whittlesea in his honour, following his success. She had, he said 'under the most extraordinary and often sanguinary circumstances, followed him to every quarter of the globe with a devotion he found difficult to describe'. He continued, she had 'watched him in the field of battle and tended to his needs in hours of pain'. When they were parted he 'regarded her as present as his guardian angel, for in difficulties and dangers he had often witnessed her shadow, as it were, in his path'.[46] Loud cheers followed when he thanked all for honouring his wife, because he knew she well deserved it. Juana's behaviour and conduct throughout the years gained her a respect and regard bordering on love from officers and men alike. The sentiments behind Harry's words were embraced as the truth. He knew without a doubt that his decision to make Juana his wife had proved to be the defining moment of his life and career.

High born though she was, Juana had not lived the sort of luxury in her life that was the norm for many of the wives accompanying their husbands on the campaign trail. Other wives, more accustomed to years of pampering and ease, found the changes almost impossible to endure and were at times more of a hindrance than a support to their husbands, their neediness providing extra worries and concerns. Juana's youth was an additional enabling factor in her endurance of harsh conditions imposed by accompanying the men into battle. A 14-year-old has less awareness of their own mortality than those more advanced in years.

Stories of a folkloric quality abounded of how, for example, she was content to sleep on the battlefield with fresh-cut wheat for a mattress and how the following morning her horse, who she had held on to all night, 'ate all her bed from under her'.[47] In another instance, after a night long soaking and sleeping in 'a little hole about six foot square', with all their greyhounds, when Harry returned from various duties, he found 'the young wife as neat as a new pin in her little tent, her habit and all her things which had got wet in yesterday's rain hung out to dry'.[48] Harry was sure that 'Blackguards as many of these poor fellows were, there was not a man who would not lay down his life to defend her.'[49]

She was never squeamish in the face of the terrible traumas and injuries she witnessed, her first concern always to assist and comfort the afflicted however dreadful their wounds. There are reports of her, not yet 16, riding over the battlefields, covered with dead, dying and wounded, tending to as many as she could.

On 17 November 1812 during the retreat from the occupation of Madrid, Harry commanded the turbulent River Huebr crossing, and left Juana in the care of the 52nd, about to make camp for the night. The 52nd were immediately ordered into action to prevent a flanking movement. Juana had no option other than to follow on her horse Tiny, a small Arab, into the fast-flowing current. Men and horses perished, but Juana clung to Tiny and made it across: 'The torrential rain was incessant: the mules had gone astray' and 'the billet that night was merely a seat on the ground and no shelter from the wet'.[50] Harry eventually found her, admitting to fellow officers that he 'felt sorry for this delicate young creature . . . wet as a drowned rat, with nothing to eat and no cover from the deluge'.[51] Juana may have been young and slightly built, but delicate she most certainly was not, as the years ahead were to prove. Years later Harry told Juana, 'Oh, how I pitied you some days, although I never said so.'[52] Pity was not a word that Juana would have willingly embraced, at any age.

Often, all they had for shelter at night would be a barn shared with their horses and whatever other animals were in residence at the time. After the battle of Vitoria in June 1813, following one such night in agricultural discomfort, Juana heard the moans of a wounded man, from the hay loft above them. It was discovered that twenty French officers injured in varying degrees of severity had been laid there all night, and one near death, were being tended by a sorrowful Spanish lady. Juana breached the communication barrier and busied herself sharing their own meagre food supplies and medical help with their erstwhile enemies.

Since the siege at Badajoz, Juana had marched 500 miles with the army. According to those around her she appeared to have 'enjoyed every day of it and was never sick or sorry',[53] even when she broke her foot, having been pinned to the ground by the lamed thoroughbred mare she was riding. Writhing in pain, she refused to be left behind, insisting 'Get me a mule or a donkey. Put a lady's Spanish saddle on it. My feet can rest on the footboard, for go with army I will.' Such was her popularity that dozens of officers hurried off, all eager to be the one to provide for her comfort. After the next day's march, there was a 'levee of officers by the mule, all laying their cloaks on the ground', to enable Juana to dismount with minimal discomfort.[54]

Juana, as all the wives, had to live each day of battle in a state of anxiety as to the safety of her beloved husband. Juana, never content to simply sit and wait, would often spend her days following up the battle on horseback. There was little in the way of creature comforts during such times. Sleeping rough on straw in draughty barns, without light or food was commonplace. The reality of 'following the drum' was devoid of any romantic notion that might have been associated with the concept. Despite her fondness for fine gowns, Juana could be practical and thrifty when times called for it. They abandoned some of their baggage and stores on a long march, rather than exhaust the bullocks carrying them. Harry commented on their arrival at the next town, Salamanca, 'My wife, with the foresight of age rather than youth, expended some of the doubloons in buying me two pairs of worsted stockings and a pair of worsted mitts and the same for herself.'[55] This was a sound investment for the rains that followed.

Juana's courage went beyond that of simple endurance. During a night march in relentless rain, the column lost its way, trying to locate the bridge over the Arragon. Juana's horse, Tiny, went lame once more, and Juana, still suffering pain from her previous foot injury, was forced to dismount, and crawl on all fours over rocky roads. Harry was involved in the search for the bridge and was unaware of his wife's predicament. When he eventually found her, she was sitting on the ground, holding her own umbrella, not to shelter herself, but to protect the rheumatic General Vandeleur. She was reported as treating the whole thing as a huge joke. She never willingly allowed her own discomfort to inconvenience others, although many officers vied to help her at any opportunity. Her behaviour and determination also enhanced the standing of Harry in the eyes of both his subordinates and commanding officers. In the years to come he expressed 'his gratitude to God for the wife that had been given him'.[56]

The fluctuation between times of luxury and periods of privation, combined with the lack of notice for a new posting, sometimes as little as one or two days, made life difficult and unpredictable. In July 1828, Harry was given a posting to Jamaica as Deputy Quartermaster General with the rank of Lieutenant Colonel. Here they faced dangers as deadly as any that were to be faced in combat. Soon after they had landed, yellow fever claimed the lives of the entire crew they had sailed with. There was much to do to transform the soldiers' living conditions to more acceptable standards of hygiene, especially with regard to clean bedding on beds raised above floor level.

This did not address the continuing villain of the piece, the virulent and deadly yellow fever. In six weeks it caused the deaths of 22 officers and 668 men. With the Governor away, Harry was left to deal with the worsening situation, not without risk to himself and Juana. Their main strategy was to move the whole barracks to a bivouac camp in the countryside away from the overcrowded town. This had the desired effect and the numbers of sick were drastically reduced. Juana remained at Harry's side during this operation, and worked selflessly, visiting the sick and encouraging despairing soldiers, not knowing whether she would be the next victim of the terrible disease. She set up convalescent centres for those recovering, enabling them to return to full strength before returning to active service.

In January 1829, Harry received news that he had been appointed Deputy Quartermaster General at the Cape of Good Hope, to leave within forty-eight hours. This was an extremely welcome posting. Harry was so secure in the knowledge that his wife would support him, saying of her, 'She begs me to say that she can campaign as well as ever.'[57] Harry rarely had to worry about Juana's reaction to the prospect of any upheaval.

Within forty-eight hours, they had sold all their household possessions, carriages and horses, and were on their way to board the first ship available to cross the Atlantic. Their patience was tested, as it took nearly one month to secure a passage to Liverpool on the brig *Euphemia*, which 'sailed like a witch'[58] through the roughest seas imaginable. By all accounts this month long journey may have surpassed all previous suffering on or off the battlefield. Harry and Juana, forced to share a cabin with other officers, were battened down for safety for the most part, and had little to eat except some provisions that Harry had brought aboard. Cockroaches swarmed all over them as they tried to sleep. It was so cold that many sailors' hands became afflicted by frostbite, and there was no 'grog' aboard to alleviate the physical and mental torment of the crew.

Harry and Juana responded valiantly by sharing with them their own meagre supply from a small cask of rum. Harry was later to describe the captain of the brig as an 'ignorant brute, without the foggiest notion of where they were'.[59] He nearly collided with a small Irish fishing boat, the skipper of which directed them towards the Mersey. Their survival hung on their ability as a couple to endure such hardship, but for Juana, as always, what really mattered was that she was with her beloved Harry. This constant endurance and lightness of spirit may at times have been a lifesaver for both of them. If experiences of her on the field of battle are a witness to her character, she would certainly have put her concern for others' welfare above that of her own comfort during this terrible voyage. After docking at Liverpool, they were accommodated at the Adelphi Hotel. Juana, always able to live in the present moment, was immediately able to perform the duties required of her without recourse to a lengthy period of recovery.

At the age of 45, Juana's courage and ability to play a major role in campaigns had not diminished. During their time in India on 29 December 1843, in the Battle of Maharajpore, Harry rode out with Sir Hugh Gough at the head of 12,000 troops to engage with the enemy, seen by Harry on a reconnaissance mission the previous day. They left before dawn, leaving those remaining in camp, the Governor General (Lord Ellenborough), lady followers and other civilian onlookers hoping to enjoy a leisurely breakfast. They were taken completely by surprise when roundshot began to bombard the British, the enemy having advanced under cover of darkness to occupy the village of Maharajpore. Until that point Ellenborough had believed they were in a safe position and that he would be perfectly placed to encourage his men to engage the enemy. Instead he suffered the humiliation of his troops watching as he retreated to safety as the enemy guns concentrated their first attention on these rear batteries.

To avoid dust clouds from the battlefield, the ladies were all riding elephants, and enjoying the sense of having a wonderful view of the scene, whilst chatting amiably amongst themselves. At this point they came under attack, 'cannon balls bowling towards them and between their elephants' legs'. Juana 'as an old soldier' immediately took command of the situation. She later complained that 'the conduct of the feminine contingent was anything but satisfactory'. Juana remained calm and in control of her companions, most much younger and fitter than herself but in danger of becoming hysterical with panic. She led them to safety, with no dependence on anything other than her own exceptional leadership and calming qualities.

Juana never bothered the men to assist her in her troubles, believing that they had quite enough to contend with without having to worry about a group of helpless females. The only casualty was one of the elephants, who lost part of an ear due to an exploding magazine. It is reported to have 'bounded off with amazing speed'.[60] In the ensuing lull, the ladies were able to view the aftermath of battle, completely devoid of romantic images of flashing steel and glorious victors. They witnessed the 'mangled remains of men, dashed to eternity', and listened to the groans of amputees in hospital tents, surrounded by piles of recently strong and healthy limbs. A sombre air pervaded their tent, where they sipped tea and spoke in whispers. They believed the carnage to be over, but following a burst of explosions, soldiers rushed in and pulled them out with seconds to spare, before a large mine exploded and their tent was blown to pieces.

A nerve-shattering night punctuated by the 'dull heavy sounds of mines exploding',[61] made all grateful to see the dawn. Sir Charles Napier, the Commander-in-Chief in Bombay, wrote a sarcastic letter of congratulation to Harry on the victory, but speculated that the presence of the ladies had been due to the fact that they had 'all wanted to be gloriously rid of their wives!' He added that, due to the alleged indiscretions of some of their menfolk, the ladies may have reciprocated this desire to their husband's fate. 'God forgive you all,' he concluded, 'Read your Bible and wear your laurels.'[62]

News of Juana's acts of selfless courage reached the ear of Queen Victoria. She awarded Juana a special medal for her bravery, and Harry wrote home declaring 'Juana is again a heroine'.[63] Following the victory at Maharajpore, Harry was made Knight Commander of the Most Honourable Military Order of the Bath (KCB). He requested his sister Alice to 'Remember I am Sir *Harry* Smith – none of your Henries.'[64] He also insisted that Juana be addressed as Lady Harry Smith or Lady Wakelyn Smith, as he felt that plain Lady Smith to be 'like a title in a bad farce'.[65] It could be argued that his main motive was to have himself included in the honour each time she was addressed. He was often aware that her appeal overshadowed his own, despite his overwhelming love for her.

Her childhood in one of the old aristocratic Spanish families imbued her with the ability to mix with adults in a socially-acceptable manner. Their household had often been visited by Wellington and his officers. These included Lord Fitzroy Somerset, the future Lord Raglan, and she was known to Wellington who 'gave away the little bride'.[66] This stamp of approval may have initiated the respect she was able to command, but it was her own charm that allowed this to develop into a devotion entirely of her own making. Despite the initial reservations of many, Juana soon became the 'darling of the whole division'.[67] By the time they had left Badajoz, 'Every man in the Light Division came to love Juana. They looked upon her as their mascot.'[68] Mature beyond her years, she was a natural communicator. She 'would laugh and talk with all, which a soldier loves',[69] in a way that was not seen as precocious or coquettish. She was too firmly in love with Harry for indiscretions of any kind and her newly-acquired broken English charmed all around her. She never felt that any task was beneath her dignity and when the need arose was more than willing to 'cook all day long'.[70] Kinkaid, Harry's silent rival in love, recalled the time she simply pressed her hand into his to allay his fears for the forthcoming battle. For the rest of the day he said he 'felt a lightness of heart and a buoyancy of spirit, which in such a situation was no less new than delightful'.[71] He proclaimed her, and many agreed 'a pattern to her sex and everybody's beau ideal of what a wife should be'. All this in praise of a 14-year-old girl.

As time progressed, Juana continued making an impression on those around her, including royalty both British and foreign, and those of higher rank than her husband. The Duke of Wellington remained as enchanted with her as he had originally been, using her Christian name when addressing her. During their time at Cambrai from 1816 to 1818 Harry recalls that his wife was 'feted and petted by everyone'.[72] Juana was more than able to uphold her place in all social circles, a quality which was to stand her in good stead when, between campaigns, they were invited to a 'continual round of balls, agreeable parties, and amateur theatricals'.[73] Juana was naturally blessed in all the attributes required for such a life, and her outstanding qualities were reflected in the goodwill shown to her husband, rather than vice versa. Hearing her sing at one occasion, her voice was likened to the 'last sigh of a dying angel'. A curious comparison but in its time, highly complementary. She was known for her ability to relate a tale with enormous vivacity, 'her dark eyes flashing and her long fingers flourishing about',[74] a sharp contrast to the pale, more reserved British wives, an exotic flower in a field of daisies.

At a ball attended by the Russian Prince and Princess Narinska, Wellington requested that a Mazurka be danced. All ladies but the Russian princess remained seated, being unfamiliar with the steps and unwilling to look foolish. Wellington approached Juana, took her hand and led her on to the dancefloor, where he handed her to an eager young Russian officer. There may have been many watching, who wished the young favourite Spanish heroine would trip over her feet but Juana, as always, rose to the occasion and danced as perfectly as if it had been her national dance. During that evening the Grand Duke Michael also waltzed with her. Wellington introduced her to Tsar Alexander I of Russia, who was most impressed when this young girl was able to converse in fluent French with him on matters of war, on a par with any knowledgeable field officer. Harry was only able to share a fraction of the limelight, and may have been torn between enormous pride and an understandable irksomeness at her ability to outshine him. In November 1826, in Nova Scotia, Harry was made Deputy Quartermaster General in Jamaica. At their triumphal embarkation in Halifax, the procession aboard was led by the governor, with Juana's arm tucked into his. She was not known ever to have pushed herself forward, but was always sought out to take centre stage, over her less charismatic husband.

Juana, even at 16, was never one to take advantage, and sought to rectify any action that may cause distress to another. Following an act of kindness by a widow, who had served them food from a valuable Sèvres bowl, Juana's groom, mistakenly or otherwise, took the bowl to serve his mistress's breakfast milk next day when they had travelled on. Juana was furious with him and determined to return it to the widow. She did so on the pretext of 'going to see an officer who had been wounded the day before yesterday'.[75] This is a rare instance of Juana deceiving her husband, displaying her strong sense that a wrong must be righted. To his credit, Harry does not seem to have been angry with her despite the fact that she was in real danger of being taken prisoner by a French patrol. 'He never controlled her desire on such occasions, having perfect confidence in her superior sense, and seeing her frequently visit our wounded and sick.'

During the Sixth Frontier War in 1835, Harry worked to keep the army fit for war by day, but by his own admission needed Juana's help to establish a suitable social life for the evenings. There were clashes of personalities and policies that made socialising likely to end in quarrels. It was the presence and tact of Juana that kept precarious situations from erupting into unpleasantness. Harry had a tendency to speak his mind and act accordingly, which in itself needed careful handling. Juana was the instrument of calming him and pouring oil on troubled waters. She utilised this gift when Harry had the difficult task of pacifying the Xhosa. The danger to them was particularly acute when Harry and Juana had to sleep in temporary tents while their house was being completed. It became necessary for them to be guarded day and night by sentries. With a stroke of brilliance, Juana, took the issue into her work with the wives of the Xhosa, whom it is suggested she persuaded to 'curb their men's brutal and warlike tendencies'.[76] This initiative may have played a major part in eventually establishing peace in September 1835.

Harry continued to be a devoted husband, realizing his good fortune in being married to this shining star, who undoubtedly had a positive effect on his career. Harry never had the slightest anxiety that Juana would let him down, even on such an auspicious occasion as a dinner in May 1847, attended by the Queen, the Duchess of Kent, the Dukes of Wellington, Montrose and Beaufort, the Earl of Ripon, the Lord Mayor of London and Sir Robert Peel. Over the years, Smith somehow became able to convince himself that crowds turned out to cheer them solely due to *his* successes and triumphs. He took it for granted that in 1835, the Boer families received Juana with wonderful hospitality, during her journey to join him when travelling from Cape Town to King William's Town, purely on account of most of the men being under his command and his popularity with them. The following year, when he and Juana returned to Cape Town along the same route, he was sure that 'in every town they passed through, every Boer turned out to meet *him*'.[77] Juana was never recorded as resenting this, so devoted was she to her husband.

Throughout the horrors and difficulties of following the camp, Juana, unlike many of those around her remained unchanged in spirit. She provided 'an escape from harsh reality', for Harry and those around them, with her 'playful and gentle manners, her open and unfettered personality, always guaranteed to lift spirits'.[78] Fatigue and discomfort never resulted in despair, and despite her unswerving devotion to Harry, her presence was deeply affecting to others, as Kincaid, the early rival in love who never relinquished his regard for her, testified, 'The friendship of man is one thing – the friendship of woman another, and only those who have been on the theatre of fierce warfare, and knowing that such a being was on the spot, watching with earnest and unceasing solicitude over his safety, alike with those most dear to her, can fully appreciate the additional value which it gives to one's existence.'[79] Kincaid was clearly still in love with Juana, and rightly believed that he held a special place in her heart. It is this which inspired him to persevere in battle, almost as if she had been his own wife. Kincaid remained a bachelor all his life. Perhaps he felt that no other woman could match the qualities he saw in Juana.

At the end of his soldiering Sir Harry Smith was still employed in 'shelving billets'.[80] He died at the age of 74 on 12 October 1860. Juana survived him, passionately cherishing his memory, and speaking of him with unerring fondness. Twelve years later, almost to the day, she died on 10 October 1872. They rest side-by-side in the cemetery at Whittlesey, having shown in their lives an example of devotion and true comradeship rare for their time.

For many years veterans of the siege of Ladysmith during the South African War of 1899 to 1902 were urged at reunions to 'drink in silence to the memory of absent comrades, and spare a thought for that gallant little Spanish girl who soldiered so manfully and from whom the town you fought for got its name – Juana Maria de los Dolores de Leon'.[81]

Chapter 4

'The Heroine of Cabul': Florentia Sale

It says a great deal about the character of Florentia Sale that, prior to accompanying her husband Major General Sir Robert 'Fighting Bob' Sale on the campaign to Kabul in Afghanistan in the summer of 1841, when asked what she would like to take with her, she specified her grand piano, seeds for English blooms and vegetables, and her youngest, 'winsome' daughter, Alexandrina.

On 6 January 1842 the British were forced to retreat from Kabul. Florentia's greatest regret was that she would have to leave behind her excellent kitchen garden.[1] She tried to harvest as many of the edible plants as possible to supplement their rations on the journey ahead. It is astonishing that in rugged mountainous terrain, with limited rainfall, most of the English seeds had thrived under Florentia's care. It was extraordinary that she would even have contemplated bringing such things to a particularly inhospitable war zone, but she had a fierce determination to make life as tolerable as possible for herself and others. Her grand piano was also to be abandoned, but the 'winsome' daughter was not so fortunate. Her husband, full of misplaced bravado, had assured her they only had to knock down a few forts when he led his brigade off to Jalalabad on 11 October 1841. He had left Florentia in Kabul, expecting her follow in three to four days.[2]

Florentia Wynch was born on 13 August 1790, in Madras. In 1809 she married Robert Henry Sale, a British army officer serving in India. Dubbed 'the Grenadier in Petticoats', she accompanied him on his numerous postings, including Mauritius, Burma, India and Afghanistan, raising their twelve children – four died in infancy and a fifth in childhood – while he fought. During the First Anglo-Afghan War, Lady Sale, along with other women and children as well as a few officers, was held captive for nine months. The group was taken hostage by Akbar Khan following the massacre three days after the retreating army had been attacked in the Khoord-Kabul Pass. Amongst the hostages with Lady Sale were her youngest daughter Alexandrina and her new-born granddaughter.

Throughout her time as a captive, Lady Sale kept a diary, which she had begun in September 1841, detailing the events of the ordeal. Published in 1843, the account read and repeated most intently by the public was that of the 'Heroine of Cabul'.[3] Her celebrity status, a decade before war correspondents reported from the front lines, meant that her words were circulated widely and read avidly. She had a powerful hold on the national consciousness and was central to the narrative of the First Anglo-Afghan War.

Naturally enough, her journals did not portray Florentia as others saw her. She was widely acknowledged as formidable. Sir Henry Hardinge, who was to become Governor General of India as a result of the war, wrote to his wife from Calcutta in January, 'I have invited Sir Robert Sale, Lady Sale, Mrs Sturt and children to take up residence here. Lady Sale is a clever woman, shrewd enough to be on her guard in society, but from what I hear, very coarse.'[4] The Sales had come out to India from home leave on the same steamer that took Hardinge to his new appointment. Writing to his stepson's daughter a few days after writing to his wife, Hardinge again commented, 'Heroines ought to be eccentric, but Florentia coming out with a direct plain oath is in proof of a maxim of mine, that ship-board tries the temperament so boisterously, that nature is displayed before the passage is at an end.'[5] The arrival of 'Major General Sir Robert Sale and the equally heroic Lady Sale and her widowed daughter Mrs. Sturt and child' at Lyme Regis had been reported by *The Times* in July 1844 and Robert and Florentia had been received by the Queen.[6]

Florentia Sale made it plain in the introduction to her journals that she not only noted down events at the end of the day, but often wrote hourly, made possible because she kept her notes in a bag permanently tied tightly round her waist.[7]

Temperatures were often well below zero at the beginning of the Afghan winter and the journey was made more difficult because of large stones in the road. The officers blazed a terrifying trail, as the enemy concealed behind rocks were able to pick off many men, and appeared to target officers in particular. Florentia understood that direct communication with her husband would be rare. She had an excellent grasp of the most complex situations, despite the differing tribes and factions involved in the conflict. On 29 October she received information that en route to Jalalabad her husband's party had been forced to march continually as the rearguard had been attacked daily and their tents fired on every night. She was particularly horrified on hearing the news that the camels were dying at the rate of forty per night of cold and starvation, rare for such hardy creatures.

On 2 November her son-in-law Sturt was brought into the camp with horrific injuries. It was through the steadfast care of Florentia and her daughter during the night that he survived and was eventually restored to his unit, only to be mortally wounded two months later. Florentia recorded that her way of coping during this period of her life when any moment could be her last, was to 'shut our eyes to our probable fate'.[8] This quality no doubt served her well when on 3 November there was 'great talk of the Kohistanees being expected to arrive to attack us'.[9] She noted with a bleak honesty that 'no military steps have been taken to suppress the insurrection, nor even to protect our only means of subsistence in the event of a siege'. Then came news that 'the city is about to be fired'.[10] Nothing else; no mention of fear. Throughout, she has a propensity to record life-threatening events in a calm and matter of fact way. 'The enemy are using our guns against us' and 'there is a report we are to be attacked in cantonments tonight'. All pass with no comment. While she scribbled away, she had no idea what was going to happen in the next hour. It was noted by those around her that neither her demeanour nor expression gave away her emotions.

Never one to sit around idly or hide in a corner by dint of being a woman, Florentia frequently joined in the throwing of shells in the early hours, to create confusion amongst the enemy. She made it her business to pick up some of the local slang. For example, she knew that when someone was referred to as 'gobrowed' that they were something between dumbfounded and at their wits' end.[11] Her published journal had a full vocabulary of Afghan and other words to guide the reader.[12]

Florentia was incredibly observant, noting that one of the advantages the Afghans had over the British and Indian troops consisted in dropping their men fresh for combat; each horseman would take a foot soldier up behind him, and drop him when he arrived at the spot he was required to fire from. She noted too that their horses 'scrambled about like goats', unlike their own rather shambling steeds, more used to level paths.[13] Florentia occasionally belittled herself and noted something 'being so clearly explained that even I understood it as well as hemming the handkerchief I was making'.[14] The fact that she even took time to hem a handkerchief is extraordinary in itself.

Florentia was quick to notice flaws in important decisions. She was particularly aggravated when, despite her opposition, camp was made too far from good water and in a spot commanded by the mountains that surrounded it, making it easier for the enemy to pick them off. She detected incompetence, especially when, with a little foresight, she had felt that dangerous situations could be avoided. She could not understand why vital medicines and medical equipment, not heavy to carry, had not travelled with the troops. This in her opinion, could have avoided long waits by the sick and injured for treatment which could have saved lives and averted unnecessary suffering. Her criticisms were not usually because of her own discomforts, but on account of the suffering of others. She saw such errors as failing to hold the so-called Commissariat Fort and the husbanding of artillery ammunition when there was more than enough for a twelve-month siege.[15]

When a force of about 3,000 showed itself on the mountains, as she had feared they would, in desperation she threw shell fragments at them, causing significant injuries. There is always an underlying sentiment in her journals that she would rather die active than cowering. During the siege of Kabul, Florentia never slept until daylight and sat up night after night to watch events as they unfolded and to give the alarm if need be.[16]

She frequently mentioned in her journal her own opinions of various officers. They vary from 'he possesses much personal bravery', to her view of the commanding general, Major General William Elphinstone, 'who vacillates on every point'.[17] She was not to know the effects and chaos these entries would have when read in England, where the aged Elphinstone was widely criticised for his incompetence.

Florentia possessed a phenomenal memory for intricate details of strategic manoeuvres. She was never less than honest, and admitted that when their troops bombarded Kabul from the cantonments, 'the effect was beautiful, but the land and number of victims from so great an expenditure of ammunition was very small'.[18]

At times of frantic action Florentia often spoke as 'we' this and 'we' that is if she was one of the men, and not in need of special protection, like many of the other women. On 13 November, when seeing troops charged furiously by the Afghan cavalry, she recorded a rare account of her feelings, and even this is embellished with wonderfully descriptive writing. 'My very heart felt as if it leapt to my teeth when I saw the Afghans charging at us . . . They looked like a great cluster of bees, but we beat them and drove them up again.'[19] She could only have seen them like this due to her usual but hazardous viewpoint on the roof of a house.

Her letters to Sale were sometimes the only details of events he had received. She could adopt a mocking and sarcastic tone, particularly noticeable in her opinion of one particular plan. She wrote, 'Our plan was to sally forth, sword in hand and attack the town, a measure that must have been attended with great loss on our side, even if victorious; with a pleasing certainty of all that were left in cantonments having their throats cut during the absence of the troops.'[20]

On 21 November, unusually for her, Florentia was unnerved by the fact that the enemy were 'uncommonly quiet'.[21] Able to watch events unfold from her place on the roof, the lack of action caused her to fear that the foe were engaged in forming new and deadly plans of attack. Some of the officers seemed to take pleasure in relating gruesome details of past Afghan atrocities, and their methods of killing and maiming their enemies. This she felt was an unnecessary addition to the anxiety already experienced by the troops as they awaited their next call to action. She criticised the officers for this, as she felt it could be detrimental to the men if their heads were full of grim possibilities. One commented, after a delivery of vital supplies of grain, 'It was needless, as we will not live to eat it.' This she thought the greatest of morale-destroyers.[22]

Florentia was also critical of those officers who chose not to share in the privations of their men, and in going on her rounds at night, another glimpse into the comprehensive role this indubitable lady played, she noticed that many of the officers were seldom found with their men. She observed that those officers who did choose to remain with their Indian troops were 'appreciated as they deserved',[23] and fought better when called to do so.

She also remarked 'Whatever we think ourselves, it is best to put a good face on the business.'[24] This trait was one that Florentia adhered to on a daily, and nightly, basis throughout the whole captivity and march, giving confidence to those around her. She identified and named in her journal, officers she considered worthy and unworthy of positive mention in this matter. The higher ranks were not missed out of her writings. Apart from Elphinstone, she also suggested of one failed sortie on 23 November, 'The misfortunes of the day are mainly attributable to [Brigadier General John] Shelton's bad generalship . . . '[25] She noted that there was such disorganization and lack of clarity in the chain of command that even a mob of large numbers of the enemy mighty beat them. On 6 December the garrison of one small fort fled from an attack that Lady Sale felt that 'a child with a stick might have repulsed'.[26]

As time went on, her remarks were peppered with increasingly dark humour, and served to ridicule those in command. Of one 'excellent' suggestion by Major Eldred Pottinger she recorded that it was to 'erect a battery on the Seeah Sung Hills (of course to be the work of fairies during the night), fire our shots from the cantonments into this battery where, of course, guardian sylphs would protect the lives of our men.'[27] Such candid remarks caused some trouble at a later date when her journals were made public.

One entry in her journal unselfconsciously speaks volumes about her courage and tenacity. She wrote on 23 November, 'I had taken up my post of observation as usual, on top of the roof of the house, whence I had a fine view of the action, and where, by keeping behind the chimneys, I escaped the bullets that continually whizzed past me.'[28] One of the 'anxious sights' she saw from this vantage point was when the enemy 'drove our men before them very like a flock of sheep with a wolf at their heels'.[29] She witnessed those she knew cut down in front of her. She saw what no-one else could have seen, but in her distress still managed to record details of the number of the enemy, the type and variety of weaponry they employed. This proved invaluable time and time again to those planning counter-attacks.

Ever practical, at daybreak she would climb down and organize breakfast for those who returned. Officers and commanding officers felt no inhibitions about discussing their plans in her presence, and may well have consulted her on such matters, not the usual procedure for a campaign wife. She rarely entered in her journal any admission of the type of hysteria normally associated with women of that era, and it is doubtful that she ever displayed in her demeanour any sign of weakness or lack of courage. A comment such as 'our situation is far from pleasant',[30] is the norm for her descriptions of events, which to most would be full of horror and foreboding. In a matter of fact way she reported the possibilities of being 'cut into mincemeat' and that 'the heads of all European officers being taken away, and no doubt exhibited as trophies'.[31] She didn't voice these fears, unlike the habit of the officers she censured. The fact that so many Afghan servants were able to walk in and out of the fort unchallenged was also a cause for concern.

Winter now had Kabul in its grip. Supplies were running low, and any attempt to leave the fort and secure some were thwarted by the constant threat of the enemy lurking about the local villages. A letter from the general to Sturt showed signs of last resort strategies. He enquired she says 'whether we had ladders, or the means of making them'. One of the horses was so hungry that it bit off and ate another's tail. Florentia remained resolute to do all she could to better their dire situation. Her journals record her opinion that 'certain it is that we have very little hope of saving our lives'.[32]

Negotiations were now underway to allow the garrison to leave Kabul and rejoin Robert Sale's force at Jalalabad. To Florentia it seemed that the refusal to follow Sturt's military advice to take the citadel of the Bala Hissar had resulted in 'the humiliating situation in which we are'.[33] But the die was cast and, despite many warnings of likely treachery, of which Florentia was well aware, an agreement was reached on 1 January 1842 for supposedly safe conduct for the garrison's withdrawal from Kabul.

For the retreat, Florentia organized for the sick not to be left, as was originally intended. Sick officers would be carried in dhoolies, which would take up horses, therefore much of the baggage had to be carried and valued possessions left behind, with no hope of any recompense. An added complication was the heavy fall of snow blocking the passes. Always blunt in her account, she wrote, 'I am not attempting to shine in rounded periods, but give everything that occurs as it comes to my knowledge.'[34] Her journal at this point indicated total chaos in the group, as different arrangements went wrong. She had the difficult task of informing two of her friends of their husbands' assassinations while negotiating with the Afghans. She felt that many on both sides were the equivalent of double agents. Contracts signed in good faith were breached, adequate provisions were not kept, and she recorded that it became impossible to know whom to trust. She quoted one captain as saying, 'I would rather put a pistol to my wife's head and shoot her rather than allow her to be taken hostage.'[35] She noted that all plans were made more difficult and more likely to be thwarted by the natural ferocity of the Afghans and their lack of compassion. Both night and day were punctuated by the sound of gunfire and bugles, 'whether we go by treaty or not, I feared but few of us will live to reach the provinces'.

She was increasingly disheartened to learn of the new decision that the sick were indeed to be left behind, and that medical men drew lots to decide who should stay to care for them. Matters were in such disarray that it became a pointless speculation upon who was actually their military chief. Things had got to such a state that no orders of any importance were transmitted in writing, so no one could really be made accountable for any actions. As the retreat approached, fit camels were forced to be exchanged for unfit camels, supplies of food were plundered and heavy falls of snow continued.

She noted that there were many less-than-clever propositions to get the retreat started, one being that they needed 250 planks to make a bridge for crossing streams. This would require 125 camels to transport them. Ever practical, Florentia questioned why they would even need planks as there was not a stream anywhere that wasn't totally frozen, and likely to remain so for the foreseeable future.[36] They had been waiting for well over a week to get marching on the retreat with plan after plan being thwarted, amended or abandoned. Florentia's diaries often indicate she felt a woman's brain might have managed the whole thing from start to finish much more satisfactorily.

She rarely heard news of her husband, but when he did write, it became plain that he had no idea what had been happening to her. He wrote that he still trusted in God that the Kandahar force would arrive in time to save them, which must have provided little comfort and assurance, in the chaos that surrounded them. There is a resigned manner about her, as she says 'the Afghans still tell us we are doomed'.[37]

In her final entry before the retreat, she recalled that three conflicting orders were given, to march out at 6am, to march at 7.00am and to march out at 8.00am. The snow was a foot deep and the temperature well below freezing. One of her last memories before starting the march was that the last dinner and breakfast were cooked over the wood of a mahogany dining table.[38] The retreating force comprised some 4,500 fighting men with an additional 12,000 native followers. Only one, Dr William Brydon, reached Jalalabad.

Although terms had been agreed, the matter of safe escort was very fragile indeed. Characteristically Florentia and her daughter chose to ride separately from the main body of ladies, and mix themselves with the troopers. The progress was unbearably slow, 2½ hours for the first mile. Their clothes became wet, and immediately froze. There would be no fresh clothes available until the end of the march. 'I do not mention this as an individual grievance but to show the inclemency of the weather and the general misery sustained,' she wrote.[39]

At one point the road was covered with men, women, and children, lying down in the snow to die. With many deserting and absconding and much being plundered, the only baggage saved was one piece of bedding. There were no tents other than two or three small ones, and no food for man or animal. It is a miracle that anyone survived that first night. On this first night, Florentia, rarely prone to sentimentality, recalled a verse from Thomas Campbell's 'Hohenlinden' that haunted her day and night,

> Few, few shall part when many meet,
> The snow shall be their winding sheet;
> And every turf beneath their feet
> Shall be a soldier's sepulchre.[40]

Shawls were snatched from mothers who were finding it difficult to carry their children, even when picking their way over the bodies of the dead, dying and wounded. They struggled across streams, wet up to the knees, pushed and shoved about by men and animals.

Everyone travelled with the expectation that if in a few hours they were not deprived of life by cold and hunger, they would fall by the knives of the Afghans. Many of the troops could scarcely hold a musket or were affected by snow blindness. Any that failed to continue were left on the road to die or be butchered. Florentia continued her journal during this time in as great detail as usual.

On 9 January 1842 Elphinstone accepted Akbar's offer to take British wives and children under his protection, a number of officers accompanying their wives. In all, the party consisted of seven officers, ten officers' wives or widows, and thirteen children. Florentia believed some of these officers had abandoned their men, but this was refuted subsequently by Colin Mackenzie, captured on 8 January, who maintained that Elphinstone had ordered it.[41] Subsequently, Elphinstone, Shelton and at least six other officers and some additional children joined the party. In keeping with the customary rigid social divide of the time, a number of captured European soldiers with two sergeants' wives and a child were housed separately.[42]

Initially, the hostages were held at a fort but then they were led back along the route taken by the retreating army and on to the fortress of Budeeabad, which they reached on 17 January 1842. Supposedly they were to be taken to Jalalabad but the fortress was some 30 miles short of it.

Sarah, Duchess of Marlborough.

John, Duke of Marlborough.

Catherine 'Kitty', Duchess of Wellington.

Arthur Wellesley, Duke of Wellington.

Juana, Lady Smith.

Louisa, Lady Wolseley.

Sir Robert Sale.

LADY ROBERTS OF KANDAHAR.

Nora, Lady Roberts.

Florentia, Lady Sale.

Dorothy, Lady Haig.

Sir Douglas Haig.

Bernard Montgomery with his son, David, 1943.

Florentia remarked of 14 January, 'we marched 24 miles'.[43] The terrain was so stony that even the camels had difficulties. She remarked, 'had we travelled under happier auspices, I should probably have been foolish enough to express fear, not having even a groom to assist me. Still I could not but admire the romantic tortuous defile passed through, being the bed of a mountain torrent.' Her indomitable spirit meant she never lost her ability to appreciate the scenery.[44] On Sunday, 16 January, Florentia, as a means of comforting those around her, organized prayers, Bible readings and worship from books that had been picked up on the field. The peace of the service was soon disrupted as gunfire and chaos ruled once more.

At Budeeabad, they were able to indulge in what must have seemed like a luxury; washing their faces properly. In her usual uncompromising manner, Florentia wrote 'the cold and the glare of the sun had three times peeled my face, from which the skin came off in strips'.[45] She found the energy to criticise the food they were given, and the fact that they had to use chapattis as plates: 'even the rice was rendered nauseous by having quantities of rancid ghee poured over it, such as in India we should have disdained to use for our lamps'.[46] What seems to have upset Florentia more than any of the dangers so far encountered was the possibility of being covered with lice: 'although my daughter and I have yet escaped, we are in fear and trembling'.[47]

During this respite, she was able to send and receive correspondence from her husband, which included the most welcome news that he was well. She received a large packet of letters both from her family in the provinces and also from England. It seems utterly impossible that such a thing should happen, but it provided a very pleasant oasis of distraction in the midst of their perpetually life-threatening situation. No longer on the march, it was not long before Florentia resumed her custom of climbing on to the top of the house, not as a lookout this time, but to hang the washing out to dry on the flat roof. She mentioned in passing, 'we dispense with starch and ironing; and in our present situation must look at everything that is useful'. On 19 February she had not been long on the roof when an earthquake shook the land. She recalled 'fortunately I succeeded in removing from my position before the roof of our room fell in with a dreadful crash, but did me no injury'. As the earthquake came down the valley it was she says 'like the action of exploding mines. I hope a soldier's wife may use a soldier's simile, for I know of nothing else to liken it to'.[48] For the rest of the night they had to endure several aftershocks, some fairly severe, and by the end of the night they were completely roofless. Florentia likened the effect of the earthquake to 'the undulatory motion of a snake in the water', and later as 'the experience of a heavy ball rolling over our heads'.[49] The aftershocks continued for several weeks and added major hardship to their deprivations. Florentia was galled by the painful irony that their temporary renewal of basic comforts was destroyed not by the enemy but by what is normally called an act of God.

Robert Sale, meanwhile, had held firm at Jalalabad with his 'illustrious garrison' and, having relieved Sale in early April, Major General George Pollock's 'Army of Retribution' was advancing further into Afghanistan, supported by another force led by Major General William Nott from Kandahar. With protracted negotiations under way about the ransom or possible release of the hostages, Florentia was displeased to have no say in the proceedings, reiterating that she included herself as one of the decision-makers in most matters.

Before they were ordered to begin a march to Jalalabad, many of their possessions were taken from them. Florentia deliberately left some bottles in a small chest of drawers. She admitted, 'I hope the Afghans will try the contents as medicine, and find them efficacious: one bottle contained nitric acid, another a strong solution of lunar caustic!'[50] She was never to know if her vengeful action had triumphed.

With the hostages being hurried westwards away from Pollock's advance, Florentia's ability to endure extremely harsh conditions during marches, mark her out as quite exceptional. Some days the only water they found was so shallow and so sandy that even their horses would not drink it. Yet she encouraged others to carry on, inspired by her example. The temperature, winter now over, was uncomfortable and unpleasant because of the heat and the constant exposure to it. Again, during these difficulties, she took the time to observe tulips, mistletoe, myrrh, purple iris and amaryllis, which she noted, 'quite scented the air with a perfume resembling that of mingled violets and wallflowers'.[51]

She was attacked with fever, but was given no time to recover, and had to suffer the misery of being soaked during continuous rain. The only discomfiture she mentioned is that she shivered as she went. At no point did she discontinue her journal, and no further mention was made of her illness, apart from the fact that on one or two days she was too weak to ride. She recalled with horror passing 'a place in front of which were dead bodies and many bones strewn about: from the blood close to its entrance, there is every reason to believe that the inhabitants were supporting life by devouring each other'.[52]

She displayed her character with some force when she wrote, 'What are our lives when compared to the honour of our country? Not that I am at all inclined to have my throat cut: on the contrary, I hope that I shall live to see the British flag once more triumphant in Afghanistan. Only let us first show them that we can conquer them, and humble their treacherous chiefs in the dust.'[53] A lady of fine manners, she hated having to eat with her fingers and drink water out of a teapot. It often seemed to be the trivial which upset her most, and the greater life-threatening incidents which she faced with most courage and endurance.

Throughout her journal, there hardly seems to have been a day without gunfire, added to by circulating reports that whenever they left, opposing forces were watching to attack them by stealth. Luxury for the travellers consisted of no more than coarse cloth, soap and tallow candles, and sour plums, pretty much inedible, but Florentia, never one to waste food, made preserves. She was always aware of the misery of those around her, especially those burdened with small children, and did everything in her power to encourage and support them, denying herself some small luxuries in order that they may find life easier for themselves.

Rumours surrounding their release came and went. Over the long months Florentia learned the art of discriminating between truth and rumour, noticing discrepancies in earlier accounts of events and subsequent later accounts of the same event. This was to be a great asset in the circumstances in which they found themselves, as so many reports from both the enemy and their own men were differently reported. She noted many occasions that when large numbers of Afghans were killed, to save face the Afghans would wildly exaggerate the size of the foe who had opposed them. On one occasion they reported that they had faced 12,000 men with extensive artillery. There had probably been a trifling minor skirmish.

She was informed in May that a letter criticising Elphinstone, which she had written from Kabul in November 1841, and which Robert had passed on to the press, was being widely discussed in Britain. Her letter was produced in the House of Commons by the Prime Minister, Sir Robert Peel, who commented it was a memorandum 'more surely indicative of a high and generous and gallant spirit, I never saw'.[54] The Commander-in-Chief in Calcutta, Sir Jasper Nicolls, had equally believed Florentia's letter more informative than anything he had received from Elphinstone.[55]

The extraordinary exchange of information by which British and Indian newspapers regularly reached the hostages led her to comment in August that:

> The editors catch at every expression, used in any letters they have read; or on any comments they hear on news from Affganistan [*sic*]. A regular controversy has arisen between one, who asserts that Lady Sale in her letters evinces a strong prepossession in favour of Mahommed Akbar Khan, and another, who thinks Lady Sale wrote, as she did, because she was a prisoner: to which the first rejoins, that he does not think Lady S. would, under any circumstances, write that which was false. *There* he is right: but I would not have written on the subject at all, unless I wrote as I thought: if people misunderstand, it is their fault and not mine. Again, they say it were better I had never written at all. Perhaps so: but it seems that details were wanting; my letters to Sale gave those; and he thought them of sufficient consequence to send them to the Governor-General and the Commander-in-Chief. They were afterwards sent to England by the former; and, if the papers tell the truth, excited some attention in the highest circles.[56]

It was an early indication of what press reporting was to become. That she felt this deeply can be seen when she said, 'Let our governors general and commanders in chief look to that; whilst I knit socks for my grandchildren:

but I have been a soldier's wife too long to sit down tamely, whilst our honour is tarnished in the sight and opinion of savages.'[57]

One of the chief irritations of captivity Florentia felt was having 'gentlemen night and day associated with us'.[58] She loathed the unremitting uncleanliness. She recalled having to go ten days before having the opportunity to change her clothes or even to take them off and put them on again having washed herself. The continuing misery of lice and fleas was a constant reminder of the contrast with the life they had left behind, and the longing to return to it. However, as usual, Florentia never lost the ability to look with admiration at the terrain and countryside through which they marched: 'Had I taken the ride for my own amusement on a good course, instead of being driven about as a captive on a sorry baggage, I should have enjoyed it very much,' she says.[59]

Reaching Bameean, the party was accommodated in what amounted to five cowsheds. There was no light in the one allocated to Florentia, but 'we soon set to and by dint of hard working with sticks and stones, until I got blistered hands we knocked two small windows out of the wall and thus obtained darkness visible'. She mentioned, however, a 'nightly visitor in the shape of the largest bug I ever saw'.[60]

This inauspicious dwelling became the place where negotiations eventually settled everything for the captives, by virtue of a signed agreement by five British officers, deemed as a sacred and binding promise. Not even this proved conclusive, as promises and counter-promises flowed to and fro. Florentia wrote to her husband and informed him of the resolution to hold out until assistance arrived, 'even should we be reduced to eating the rats and mice of which we have a grand stock'.[61] Eventually reliable intelligence was received that the enemy had been overcome and that, as Florentia triumphantly wrote, 'Akbar Khan and Mahommed Shah Khan are said to be – *nowhere!*'[62]

Upon reaching Kabul, Pollock had despatched cavalry to Bameean under Sir Richmond Shakespeare. Shakespeare arrived on 17 September 1842 to confirm, amidst all the news and final marches, that Robert, she wrote in her journal, 'had been struck by a spent ball without injury; and congratulated me on our gracious Queen's bestowal of the highest Order of the Bath upon my husband; a distinction, I believe, unparalleled in his present rank and therefore the more dearly prized'.[63] Three days later Robert Sale arrived with more cavalry. For Florentia it was 'impossible to express our feelings on Sale's approach. My daughter and myself had been so long delayed, it was actually painful, and accompanied by a choking sensation which could not obtain the relief of tears.'[64] Florentia ended her journal: 'And now my notes may end. Any further journals of mine can only be interesting to those nearly connected to me.'[65] For her, anything less than a life lived on the edge was considered mundane and not worthy of mention.

There were those who felt Florentia's account damaging to the reputation of the army and the East India Company. Other captives also published journals such as that of Lieutenant Vincent Eyre, which actually appeared before those of Florentia. With the advantage of the publication of her earlier letter in *The Times*, however, Florentia's was held to be the only contemporaneous account. Another captive, Amelia Anderson, suggested that several accounts were being kept and all involved both a degree of falsification and also of copying from each other's notes. She endeavoured to promote Eyre's account over that of Florentia, albeit anonymously in the periodical *Bentley's Miscellany*, and it is clear that there was some resentment at Lady Sale's publishing success and celebrity.[66]

Florentia's reputation, however, remained untainted. She was celebrated in song and theatrical performances. *Astley's Afghanistan Campaign*, for example, was a popular circus performance at Astley's Amphitheatre in Westminster Bridge Road, Lambeth: 'The reconstruction in heroic manner in which Lady Sale fought a double sword combat with six Afghans, whom she put to flight, drew down the loudest praise; and her beautiful sentiment that the heart of the Briton, even amidst the snows of India's icy climate, still beats warmly for his native home upon the sea-bound isle was greeted with unparalleled enthusiasm.'[67] The affecting reunion of Robert and Florentia, however, was largely unseen by many in the audience as it was staged in the prompter's box.

Robert Sale was mortally wounded at Mudki in the First Anglo–Sikh War, dying on 21 December 1845. Florentia was granted a special pension of £500 per annum. She spent her widowhood on a small estate in the Indian hills near Simla, but took a trip to the Cape of Good Hope for her health in 1853. She died at Cape Town on 6 July 1853 soon after her arrival. On her tombstone is inscribed, 'Here lies all that could die of Lady Sale.'

Chapter 5

The Power and the Glory: Late Victorian Wives

The stereotypical perception that wives merely complemented their husbands in the approved manner of domestic ideology, revolving around the concepts of women's duty and women's mission, is quite apparent in Victorian memoirs and biographies.

The autobiography of Elizabeth Thompson certainly creates such an impression. Better known as the artist Lady Butler, she managed capably, although not particularly taking pleasure in it, the entertainment expected of her at the side of Lieutenant-General Sir William Butler in appointments to such home commands as Plymouth, Aldershot, Dover and Devonport. While bringing up five children she enjoyed considerable professional success herself. She indicated in her autobiography that, when given the choice of either the Colchester or Dover commands in 1896, Butler allowed her to decide on Dover, as she found its 'history picturesque' compared to Colchester. She regretted, however, that, 'It is my misfortune that I have not the knack of small talk, so useful to official people . . .'.[1] Characteristically ungracious, the leading soldier of the Victorian age, Sir Garnet (later Field Marshal Viscount) Wolseley, who attended Butler's wedding, was unimpressed by Elizabeth Thompson: 'Poor devil I think it a very bad match he has made: such a dreadful commonly sort of people from the bride's entourage. There is nothing in my opinion to recommend it.'[2] Yet, as suggested earlier, she performed her role well alongside the pursuit of her professional career.

Similarly, Lady Napier 'filled her new role with much grace and tact' when thrown into running the large establishment and organizing the scale of entertainment expected when Robert (later Field Marshal Lord) Napier became military member of the Council of India in 1861. At just 18 she took on not only her 51-year-old husband, but also two stepdaughters close to her own age.[3]

Major General Sir Charles Callwell later recalled that the wife of the General Officer Commanding (GOC) at Woolwich in 1882, Lieutenant General the Hon. Edward Thomas Gage, 'was a popular figure in local society, the essence of hospitality, and always delighted to have her drawing room congested with visitors; but she was a real terror to talk'. Indeed, few 'could get a word in edgeways, while the General would be formed up on the sofa, scowling at his radiant better-half and muttering to himself, just loud enough for everybody to hear, "Oh, damn the woman's tongue!"'[4]

Certain appointments required that a wife have appropriate social skills. General Sir Frederick (later Field Marshal Earl) Roberts recommended Viscount Frankfort de Montmorency for the Presidency command in Calcutta in 1890 rather than William Elles. He was sure that Frankfort's wife would be an asset to society, while 'the extreme deafness of Mrs Elles is a serious drawback, as it prevents her going much into society, and would have precluded her from sharing in those social functions which are so frequent at Calcutta during the cold season'.[5]

When Sir Charles Nairne was selected for the Bombay command in 1893, the Commander-in-Chief (C-in-C) in India, Lieutenant General (later Field Marshal) Sir George White commented, 'he has a nice wife to help him in his social duties'.[6] A year earlier, Sir Henry Brackenbury had noted of Sir George White's appointment as C-in-C in India that Lady White 'is well qualified to take a lead in society, and I learnt from White that he has a good private income, which is a great advantage'.[7] Colonel William (later Field Marshal Lord) Nicholson's wife was said to be a particularly successful hostess at Simla, and so 'very stately and queenly' that she was nicknamed the 'Simla Queen Victoria'.[8]

In the case of Major General the Hon. Reginald Talbot, his appointment as GOC in Egypt in 1898 was entirely due to his wife's perceived domestic competence. Lord Cromer specifically requested Talbot, 'as I thought his wife would do the social work well – and that is really all the General here has to do'.[9] Earlier, Cromer emphasised that the 'wife question was always important, and – for reasons for which you will readily understand – is doubly so now'. In the event, Talbot himself was not a success, being somewhat egotistical and 'a first-class buck-wallah' but his wife was judged particularly good-looking.[10] Similarly, the C-in-C at the War Office, the Duke of Cambridge, had recommended either Major-General Charles Knowles or Major-General Reginald Thynne for Cairo three years earlier as both had 'very nice *wives*, an important element in this selection'.[11] Knowles was chosen on that occasion.

These supporting roles hardly confer strategic or intelligent contributions from these particular wives, but major on the specifically gender-perceived roles of women of that time, and their captivating manners and appealing appearance, whilst being able to keep house and keep smiling. As other chapters demonstrate, officers' wives who broke this mould were outstanding in all spheres of life and not only matched but outshone their male counterparts in courage, strategy and effectiveness in times of extreme duress.

There were dangers in going against the old adage that 'subalterns must not marry, captains may marry, majors should marry and colonels must marry'. Marrying while still a captain, Edward May met the Military Secretary, Sir George Harman, in the street soon afterwards. Harman remarked, 'I see you've married. I congratulate you, but you're done.' His wife's health suffered from his posting to India and, having first refused it, May decided to accept appointment as instructor (later professor) in military topography at Woolwich. Subsequently, he was left a widower with four children, but he remarried in 1895,[12] and reached the rank of major general.

Major Herbert Plumer, who had married while still a captain and soon had four children, turned down the post of military secretary to Lieutenant General Sir William Goodenough at the Cape in April 1896, 'as he felt as a married man he could not do the work satisfactorily'. He was also considering leaving the army altogether. In the event, the Matabele Revolt, that had already begun, led to Plumer being appointed to command the Matabeleland Relief Force as a temporary lieutenant colonel. It was an appointment that forged his military reputation and he ended as Field Marshal Viscount Plumer.[13]

The future General Sir Aylmer Haldane was tricked, as a subaltern, into marrying a barmaid. According to Winston Churchill in 1898, Haldane had offered 'half of all he has in the world' for a divorce, but she 'wants to be a lady'. Churchill opined, 'It is impossible that he could fill any high command with such a private life. I questioned him about her health. Excellent. I am afraid I could suggest nothing better than Murder – and there are objections to that course. Poor wretch, he is fettered for life.'[14] In fact, Haldane retired as a full general in 1925, so it seems his wife did not 'fetter' him much.

Henry Brackenbury's wife lacked tact, and he regretted having married her: she had been a widow of 31 and he had been only 21.[15] For all practical purposes Brackenbury had separated from his wife in 1872, although they never divorced. He had serious affairs, reputedly with Leila Canrobet, the wife of the French Marshal François Canrobet, and with Edith Desanges, the daughter of the well-known artist, Louis Desanges. It was Edith whom Brackenbury married soon after his first wife's death in 1905.[16] But, like Haldane, Brackenbury also reached the rank of full general.

It was certainly advantageous to have the right kind of wife. A significant factor counting against Lieutenant Walter Long, whose surrender of Lydenburg to the Boers during the Anglo-Transvaal War in March 1881 resulted in a court martial and his resignation, was that Mary Long was 'not of the position of the average "officer's lady"'.[17] Yet it was generally held that her presence and courage had been considerably more inspiring to the garrison of 'Fort Mary' than that of her husband. Subsequently, Mrs Long published an account of her experiences.[18]

Similarly, the conduct of Mrs Ethel Grimwood, whose husband, Frank, the Political Resident, was killed in the Manipur uprising in June 1891, and who also published an account of her experiences, excited some comment.[19] While she had tended the wounded when the Residency was attacked, there were doubts as to how far she had been exposed to danger.

More significantly, her personal behaviour and that of her husband were believed to have contributed to the unrest, in that his philandering with native girls had been prompted by her own infidelities.[20] William Nicholson was dismissive of her, arguing she did no more than any other woman would have done in the circumstances, and that the walls behind which she sheltered were so thick that she had been in no danger.[21] Equally, the future General Sir Neville Lyttelton told his wife that no one in India had subscribed to the fund for Mrs Grimwood, despite details going to every regiment and it being sponsored by the Prince of Wales: 'I don't know whether everything will be made public that is known about her, but she will get a bad exposé if it is.'[22]

A 'strategic' marriage was also advantageous. Major General Sir Charles MacGregor's first wife was the daughter of the influential Sir Henry Durand. The marriage, which ended with her death after four years, appears to have been extremely happy but, MacGregor still noted just a month before the marriage, 'I must say I do not care much for any supposed honour there may be in allying myself with anyone in the position of Sir H. Durand; if he was a Royal Duke I should think the same, for I am proud enough of my own name to think that no other can add luster [*sic*] to it. But I do feel proud of the prospect of being allied to such a man.'[23] Ironically, in seeking to establish her husband's reputation after his early death, MacGregor's second wife, Charlotte, all but ruined it by publishing lengthy extracts from MacGregor's uncompromising diaries. As the Rev. James Williams Adams VC put it:

> Some men talk too much to their friends; but poor old MacGregor talked too much to his diary; and it is very hard upon him that his foolish notions as a boy should be published, as well as the rather unnecessary notions that influenced him throughout his career, by his own wife under the impression that she was vindicating his character & reputation.

The future Field Marshal Sir William Robertson married the daughter of Lieutenant General Charles Palin while a lieutenant in 1894, six years after being commissioned from the ranks.[24] Equally, the future Lieutenant

General Sir Edward 'Curly' Hutton married Eleanor Paulet, the wealthy niece of the Marquis of Winchester. An additional advantage was that she understood that 'professional duty is the first consideration in all circumstances of a soldier'.[25]

For good or ill, therefore, wives were seen as significant to careers. The well-known 'crammer' (officer's tutor) and military writer Dr Thomas Miller Maguire pointedly remarked to the Akers-Douglas Committee in 1902 that female influence should be kept at a distance: 'It is an abomination that the caprice of titled feminine idlers and intriguers, or of the wives of generals, should make or mar an officer's career. The nation should put an end to this monstrosity at once.'[26]

There were other wives who readily sprang to their husband's defence in the manner of Charlotte MacGregor. Fanny, Lady Cunynghame, sister to the late C-in-C Viscount Hardinge, was incensed at the apparent slight to General Sir Arthur Cunynghame as C-in-C in South Africa by Wolseley's appointment as administrator in Natal in 1875. Not one to give up, she wrote directly to the Duke of Cambridge, while her husband was absent in Griqualand, demanding either the Gibraltar or Malta commands for Cunynghame as proof of the Duke's support. Both the Secretary of State for War, Gathorne Hardy, and the Colonial Secretary, Lord Carnarvon, became involved when her demand was revived two years later, when Cunynghame was removed from the command at the Cape after clashes with the colonial authorities. Despite being an old Crimean comrade, Cambridge felt unable to recommend Cunynghame for Malta, as he regarded it as too important a command. Cunynghame himself wrote, 'She is a good wife, and is anxious for my benefit.'[27]

As the end of the Mahdist Sudan came closer, Reginald Wingate, who had become senior colonel in June 1898, wanted to obtain a post for himself in Cairo that would have some role in the future administration of the Sudan. He asked his wife to act in his interests: 'If all goes well at Khartoum – you know my views about the future and I hope that you may perhaps be able to put them forward. We must carefully watch events and in case of necessity – I shall probably wire to you what line I want you to take.'[28] Wingate was to succeed Kitchener as Governor-General of the Sudan and Sirdar of the Egyptian Army when Kitchener was sent to South Africa in 1899, although it is not apparent what role his wife played in his success.

By contrast, Colonel the Hon. James Dormer warned his wife Ella off trying to see either the Adjutant General at the War Office, Sir Charles Ellice, or the Military Secretary, Sir Alfred Horsford, on his behalf while he was in Cyprus in 1878. He told her 'When these things are done at the proper time, & in the right way, nothing does so much harm as wives or female relatives interfering'.[29] Dormer was appalled to hear that Ella proposed to see the Quartermaster General, Sir Arthur Herbert, at the War Office in May 1884, 'for as I have told you so often before I would much rather you never bothered them, for you can only do my interests more harm than good by interviewing the officials at the Horse Guards, & I so much prefer looking after my own battles'. Just five months later he was again pleading with Ella not to press his possible candidature as Military Secretary on Whitmore and Herbert: 'Only please do not put your finger in the pie & go on bothering or writing to or calling on them.'[30]

Military wives were often said to be ambitious for their husbands, as in the case of Lady Grenfell, wife of Field Marshal Lord Grenfell, whom Evelyn Baring described in 1888 as urging her husband to 'acquire the maximum amount of glory with the minimum amount of risk'.[31] Consequently, just as political hostesses used their social power to influence those able to dispense patronage to relatives and friends, military wives sought to advance their husbands by appeals for employment on their behalf. Wolseley's correspondence contains frequent examples when he was Adjutant General and then C-in-C at the War Office in succession to the Duke of Cambridge.

Four wives in particular are worth considering in more detail, as they played contrasting roles in their husbands' careers. Field Marshal Sir Evelyn Wood's wife, Paulina, and Wolseley's wife, Louisa, could be said to have acted largely within the constraints of the prevailing ideology of domesticity. They did, however, display some independence of spirit and exercised some influence. By contrast, Sir George Colley's wife, Edith, and Frederick Roberts's wife, Nora, were far from subordinate to their husbands, and stepped well beyond the accepted bounds. As it happened, Lady Wood and Lady Colley largely failed in their endeavours, whereas Lady Wolseley and Lady Roberts succeeded.

The first of those whose efforts were not always successful was Lady Wood. Evelyn Wood married the Hon. Mary Paulina Anne Southwell, sister of the 4th Viscount Southwell and a Roman Catholic, in 1867. It was a marriage that both families opposed on religious grounds.[32] At first Paulina's brother, Viscount Southwell, forbade the marriage due to the fact that their family were Catholic and the Woods were Protestant, an often-unsurmountable obstacle. For four years Evelyn had no contact with her, and then he proposed by letter. She did not reply for a week or so, in which time Evelyn decided to embark on the Abyssinian expedition. However, when he found out that it was Sir Robert Napier leading the campaign, not Sir William Napier, who he knew well, he changed his mind and carried on with his marriage proposal. He made Paulina promise that she would not interfere with his efforts to secure a command on an overseas campaign. She agreed and they were married. The problem with religion reared its head later, when his rich Aunt Ben was handing out allowances to Wood's sisters. For Evelyn there was to be nothing, on the grounds that he was married to a Catholic. Meanwhile, Wood's frequent pursuit of monetary reward was viewed as shallow by his family, and only feeding her expensive tastes.[33]

Paulina hardly features in Wood's memoirs. However, together with Wood's sister, the novelist Anna Steele, whom Lady Wolseley regarded as an 'odious hussy' responsible for writing all Wood's speeches, Lady Wood was clearly very ambitious.[34] In October 1884, for example, Wolseley noted that Lady Wood was unpopular in Cairo, where it was believed that she was behind Wood's attempt as Sirdar to avoid being subordinated to Lieutenant General Sir Frederick Stephenson, the C-in-C in Egypt. Wolseley added that Wood lived in so much adulation from Lady Wood and Mrs Steele that it would turn anyone's head, especially as he was notoriously vain.[35] There are frequent references in Wolseley's correspondence to these two forceful women in Wood's life.

It might be suspected that Wolseley was prejudiced, having fallen out with Wood after the latter had concluded the convention with the

Boers following George Colley's death at Majuba in 1881. In a letter to Wood, Colley had alluded to the likely wrath of Lady Wood, when he was preferred over her husband for appointment to the Staff College in 1876.[36] After meeting Wood in 1879 the Queen became godmother to one of Wood's daughters. Lady Wood then entered into the Queen's confidence when Wood was abroad. She acted as a conduit between the Queen and her husband during the Egyptian campaign, although not always transmitting what she felt Wood wanted kept confidential.[37] In December 1884, however, according to Lady Wolseley, Lady Wood offended the Queen by pressing her own ideas on affairs in Egypt.[38]

Unfortunately for Wood, there was something of a problem in Paulina's disordered house. It was generally accepted that it was important for the hostess, whether political or military, to be capable of fulfilling the wife's social role. On this, Lady Wood failed. In October 1880, Wolseley complained of Wood's house at Dover being as filthy as a railway refreshment room, but with Wood himself seemingly oblivious to the noise surrounding him – he was partly deaf – and to the poor food being served.[39] Seven years later the Duke of Cambridge complained to Wolseley of an 'infamous lunch' with the Woods and later suggested Wolseley advise Wood to arrange for a better cook and attempt to create a 'better appointed home'.[40] In those times criticisms of this nature would have been attributed to lack of skills and attention solely by the wife concerned. In 1898 Wolseley reminisced about how hunger alone drove one to consume what was put on the table in Wood's home.[41]

The Duke of Cambridge's comment on the Aldershot command in 1888 was that not only was Wood too junior, but that he and Lady Wood made 'a very rough couple'.[42] Though junior to many, Wood did secure the appointment as the best military candidate. In telling his predecessor, Sir Archibald Alison, that he would send down Lady Wood to negotiate on fixings and fittings, Wood said he had no knowledge of household matters and had not even drawn a cheque since the Asante campaign of 1873–4.[43]

Wood's preferment was much to the dissatisfaction of Lady Herbert, who had coveted it for her own husband, Lieutenant General Sir Arthur Herbert.[44] The Queen's private secretary, Arthur Bigge, also noted that the wife of Wood's principal rival for Aldershot, Major General John Ross, probably possessed even greater shortcomings than the duke found in Lady Wood. There was some genuine and sharp rivalry amongst the wives with regard to the upward mobility of their husbands' careers.

It seems reasonable to assume that Wood's marriage had damaged his career, as neither Wolseley nor Cambridge were impressed by his home life. They had three sons and three daughters. Paulina died on 11 May 1891, while Wood was commanding at Aldershot. After her death Wood was deeply touched to receive forty-six letters of condolence from NCOs and private soldiers who had served under him. Perhaps significantly, Wood's most prestigious appointments as Quartermaster General and Adjutant General came after his wife's death in 1891.

In contrast to Lady Wood, Lady Wolseley largely succeeded in supporting her husband's ambitions. Louisa Erskine, whom Wolseley married in 1868, was almost certainly illegitimate, being brought up as the niece and ward of her birth father Alexander Holmes. In trying to convince the Queen that Wolseley was not a radical in politics, Sir Theodore Martin reported in October 1879 that Louisa was 'a charming person – accomplished, & reminding one of a very pretty Watteau [after the eighteenth-century French artist] in her style of beauty & dress'.[45] Louisa prided herself on having the same height and proportions of the Venus de Milo, and had a reputation for dressing well. She was well read, particularly in French literature, but was plain spoken. She moved with ease in literary circles with the likes of Edmund Gosse, Henry James, and George Du Maurier. She certainly felt herself to be at least her husband's equal.[46]

Clearly, 'Loo', as she was known to Wolseley (although his endearments also ran to the distinctly curious 'little runterfoozle'), was a more-than-capable partner to her husband. She was just as determined a character, so much so that she all but cut her daughter out of her will following a rift between the two of them in 1905. Her social role was performed only in home stations, for she declined to accompany Wolseley to overseas postings on most occasions. Her only extended tour with him, after his service in Canada ended in 1870, was briefly to Cyprus in 1879. It seems astonishing that, due to his wife's pregnancy, Wolseley turned down the prestigious offer of becoming military secretary to the Viceroy, Lord Northbrook, in 1872, the post going to Northbrook's nephew, Evelyn Baring.

In Cyprus, it would appear that Loo declined to assist Wolseley in his social duties as fully as he had anticipated.[47] Certainly, after he left the island for the South African command, she wrote bitterly to Lady Wood of being left 'to sweep up the debris'.[48] Nonetheless, Neville Lyttelton considered her an able second to Wolseley when he was C-in-C in Ireland and 'entertained very largely'.[49]

Loo had little time for Wolseley's occasional philosophical musings on the nature of fame and patriotism, accusing him of consciously composing his journals too much with posterity in mind. She was jealous of other women who seemed too friendly towards him, such as Lieutenant General Sir Baker Russell's wife, 'Pal', and the Duchess of Edinburgh, whose correspondence with Wolseley she promptly returned to the royal family after his death. In September 1884, she had complained at not receiving a letter from Wolseley, assuming he was too busy writing to 'two or three duchesses' instead.[50] Attention has been drawn to their lengthy periods of separation after 1886.[51] It says much of the nature of their relationship that after she congratulated him on his success in ending the war against Sekhukhune in South Africa in 1879, Wolseley noted it was 'the first time you have ever expressed an interest or any pleasure in any public service I have carried out'.[52]

Loo also disliked several of Wolseley's companions, notably 'black' Henry Brackenbury, whom she described as having 'that shapeless nose & oily complexion'.[53] It amused Wolseley to think of her 'peculiar dislike to that putty nose & bilious complexion'.[54] Such was her antipathy to Brackenbury that Wolseley suggested that once he could secure a Companionship of the Bath or promotion for Brackenbury, he would 'feel no compunction about cutting him from my staff whenever I go anywhere with you "in my suite"'.[55] Encountering both Wolseley and Loo in Cyprus, the young Hebert (later Field Marshal Earl) Kitchener suggested that some were saying Loo 'drives the coach'. He did not like her or Wolseley's staff.[56] At this point it is difficult to see how she was to become a positive influence on her husband's career.

Whatever her apparent shortcomings, Loo was an excellent safety-valve for her husband's professional frustrations, and she played a significant role in defending Wolseley's interests at home. In 1879, while Wolseley remained in South Africa, she was the intermediary between him and prominent Conservatives over the possibility of a peerage. Similarly, in February 1880, she was sounding out ministers on Wolseley's desire to leave the Cape. Based on her soundings, she advised Wolseley against a precipitate return. Two years later, she was again negotiating the peerage on her husband's behalf while he was still in Egypt, this time with Liberal ministers, reminding them of the failure to secure the promised peerage in the previous year; a bold approach, given how it could have been perceived.

She visited Windsor in both February and March 1885, and was passing messages to Wolseley from the Queen during the Gordon Relief Expedition. The Queen sympathized that Wolseley had failed 'for reasons he and I *know* only but too well'.[57] The Queen, who believed William Gladstone's government had unnecessarily delayed authorizing the relief expedition, told Loo that she felt Wolseley should use the strongest possible language towards the government, and even threaten to resign. In April 1885 the Secretary of State for War, Lord Hartington, sought to persuade Loo to see that Wolseley should remain in Egypt a little longer.

In 1893, it was Loo rather than Wolseley who was sounded out by the Secretary of State for War Henry Campbell-Bannerman with regard to the likelihood of Wolseley accepting the Malta command.[58] After Wolseley suffered a serious illness in 1897 she was especially protective of him. Perhaps she feared for them both should his health decline to the extent that he could no longer fulfil his elevated positions, or be passed over for future advancements. She was concerned again in the crisis month of December 1899, when she recognized that, if Wolseley resigned following Roberts's supersession of General Sir Redvers Buller in South Africa, it would be regarded as pique, yet, if he stayed, it might appear that he clung to office 'or more probably that his wife does'.[59] Loo was indignant that when Wolseley left the War Office in 1900, he did so receiving only 'scant courtesy', 'icy formality' and 'without one word of thanks or of respect'.[60] In 1917, four years after Wolseley's death, Loo had an extraordinary oratory in Wolseley's memory constructed in her grace-and-favour apartment at Hampton Court.[61]

In both 1884 and 1899 Lady Wolseley found herself besieged by women trying to get husbands or sons to the Sudan and South Africa. She called those trying to achieve an appointment to the Camel Corps for the Gordon relief expedition 'camel mammas'.[62] Clearly, it was believed she might wield some influence over Wolseley in the matter of appointments. One young officer wrote to Arthur Bigge in May 1896 that, at the recent Adjutant General's ball, subalterns had 'tumbled over each other to dance with Miss Buller & Miss Wolseley. This, they tell me is the right way, to get "selected" nowadays.'[63]

Unproven gossip going the rounds in 1897 was that Wolseley had asked his private secretary, Captain Cecil Feilden, when he was going to propose to his daughter, Frances Wolseley. Feilden replied that, while he had admiration for her, he had no intention of marrying her. Wolseley had then asked if Feilden thought he had been made private secretary on his abilities, and that he could now 'go about his business'. This piece of gossip may have caused fear amongst those favoured by the Wolseleys of how much depended on their suitability for the actual post, or their suitability as a future family member through marriage.[64]

Loo had no hesitation in pressing her daughter Frances into service when she was staying with Lady Bathurst, the daughter of Lord Glenesk, the editor of the *Morning Post*, in 1900. Loo wanted Frances to persuade Glenesk on the issue of Wolseley's pension. As a field marshal Wolseley would receive £1,300 per annum, but his good service pension of £100 would lapse when he started to draw his pension as C-in-C of £2,000, so the net gain was just £600 per annum.[65] In later years Loo and Frances became estranged. Loo died in 1920.

In reality, there is little to suggest that Loo was at all influential in terms of the selection of officers or in guiding particular decisions by her husband. In that sense, Wolseley was very much his own man and, therefore, Lady Wolseley largely operated within the private sphere. There was also clearly subordination of her own role to that of her husband. However, this did not prevent her from exercising independence on occasions, nor from being influential in shaping his career in a way that at best could be termed subtle, and at worst, interfering.

Of the two women who more clearly stepped beyond the private sphere and subordination, Lady Colley certainly failed to realize fully her ambitions for her husband. George Colley's engagement and marriage at the age of 43 to the 29-year-old Edith Hamilton, daughter of Major General Henry Meade 'Tiger' Hamilton, in 1878 came as a surprise to most at Simla, where Colley was military and subsequently private secretary to the Viceroy of India, Lord Lytton.[66] Edith was regarded as 'so intelligent, nice looking, & sympathizing', if unfortunately very delicate.[67] When he was Governor and C-in-C in Natal, Colley was to write that his wife 'seconds me splendidly, and rows or laughs at the people who come to her with long faces or absurd stories'.[68] Yet, as Wood confided to the Queen just before Colley's death at Majuba, Edith's ambition for Colley 'obliterates apparently every thought of the personal danger which he has undergone'.[69]

It had been remarked that when the first train arrived in Pietermaritzburg in October 1880, while Colley stood on the footplate, Edith was literally at the engine's throttle and, thus, symbolically in control of her husband's destiny. It was also said that she had written to Colley after his defeats at Laing's Nek and Ingogo to urge him into further action, the letter mysteriously disappearing after his death. No such letter has ever been traced, although it was supposedly found on his body.[70] There are also verified letters from Edith Colley to her husband on both 15 and 24 February expressing concern for his safe return.[71] Whatever the truth, she played the part of widow to the full and it was eventually Wolseley's belief that she had married Colley as a matter of convenience rather than love. It was a conclusion reached in the light of her second marriage in 1888 and, swift and financially productive, separation in 1891 from Wentworth Beaumont, the Liberal MP for Tyneside, later 1st Baron Allendale.[72]

Turning to Roberts, in August 1900 he was C-in-C of the British forces in South Africa when he received a telegram from the Secretary of State for War, the Marquis of Lansdowne. It conveyed the Queen's concern at the presence of Lady Roberts in Pretoria. Lansdowne presented that concern to Roberts purely as a matter of the Queen's fears about the safety of his wife in the occupied former capital of the Transvaal.[73] Lansdowne, however, was concealing the Queen's real objection, as stated by her private secretary Arthur Bigge: 'Endless stories, probably many of which are untrue, reach the Queen respecting Lady Roberts' interference and her influence, even exerted on the careers of officers in high command in South Africa.' Believing that public confidence in the man most likely to be the next C-in-C at home might be shaken by the rumours, the Queen's conclusion was that, if Lady Roberts 'was *not* at Head Quarters there could be no possible ground for the accusations which are but too common against her'.[74]

Lansdowne argued that Lady Roberts would be able to nurse Roberts if he became ill again, as he had a touch of dysentery, and that Roberts had not wanted to leave her at Bloemfontein. Roberts also suggested to the Queen that his wife had been under a heavy strain through being at Bloemfontein with his daughters during a typhoid epidemic, and that he wanted her to help organize hospitals at Pretoria.[75] The Queen's intervention regarding ladies coming out 'when only inclined to spread hysterical rumours' became generally known, one staff officer remarking that 'this coming as it did immediately after Lady Roberts's arrival was to say the least of it rather pointed'.[76]

Roberts, at the comparatively young age of 27, had married Nora Bews, youngest daughter of a retired Scottish soldier, in 1859. She was just 20. She was taller than the diminutive Roberts and, according to Wolseley, when he met her for the first time in 1895, she was 'the commonest and most vulgar looking old thing I have ever met'. On the same day in a separate letter, Wolseley also remarked, 'My eyes, what a women. I have never seen a more hideous animal in my life.'[77] Thereafter, Wolseley always referred to Nora as vulgar and frumpy, writing to his brother, George, 'India to me is & has always been the home of military jobs. Roberts, instead of reforming the system, took his frumply [*sic*] vulgar old wife into partnership in business & made it worse than ever.'[78] He also alluded to her being a 'spur' in Roberts' side and, writing on his own retirement to be succeeded as C-in-C at the War Office by Roberts, Wolseley remarked that he was clearing his office 'where she can job & dispense favours to her heart's content, dreadful woman'.[79] The animosity does not seem to have been shared by Louisa Wolseley. Nora Roberts wrote on one occasion that Loo, whom she liked, had visited her while Wolseley was absent from London.[80]

Obviously, as with Wolseley's view of Lady Wood, his impartiality might be questioned. There is other evidence, however, suggesting that Wolseley was not alone in viewing Lady Roberts as a formidable woman enjoying much influence and exercising real power over her husband. General Sir George Higginson once reported to Loo Wolseley that even Lansdowne had made fun of Lady Roberts's vulgarity.[81] She appeared to the Duke of Cambridge's nephew, Prince Adolphus of Teck, as an 'awful female' who frightened everyone. Teck also referred to Roberts as 'Sir Jobs'.[82]

In August 1893 Roberts wrote to Sir John Cowell on hearing that the Queen believed he had 'been influenced by Lady Roberts in making appointments'. He acknowledged, 'I have consulted her freely on almost every subject, and she has been to me (as I imagine a good wife is to every husband) the greatest possible assistance. But', he went on, 'The only one subject which we have never discussed is that of an official appointment before it was made, in order that she might truthfully reply to the letters she occasionally received, requesting her to use her influence with me, that she knew nothing about such matters and never interfered in them.' He also claimed that Lady Roberts held strong views about the unsuitability of ladies 'going out of their own sphere', but suggested Nora had made enemies in trying to keep society in India 'correct'. Unpleasant remarks in a 'low society paper' did not trouble him, but if the Queen believed it then it was a serious matter.[83] Clearly the Queen was not reassured, for when Roberts was an outside choice for C-in-C at the War Office in 1895, she wrote both that Roberts was 'ruled by his wife who is a terrible jobber', and that his candidature was impossible 'on account of his readiness to listen to his wife, & her notorious favouritism'.[84]

Similarly, Hugh Bixby Luard of the Indian Medical Service wrote in his reminiscences that 'it was said that any ambitious officer who wished to get on found it advisable to get favour from Lady Roberts at Simla, who was supposed to have unbounded influence with him [Roberts], and was a person of very strong character'. Luard suggested, however, that Roberts had good judgement and 'exercised the same discretion in considering Lady Robert's candidates or favourites'.[85] Major General Granville Egerton recalled in his memoirs that the 'sobriquet attached to the pair in India, of Sir Bobs and Lady Jobs, was not undeserved'.[86] Sir George White also wrote of Nora Roberts's influence in July 1888, characterizing her as 'a prejudiced woman & nothing is too bad for those she does not like, but I think she is a warm friend. One thing is certain, that she takes too much part in Sir Fred's business and that it is generally known.'[87]

The young Henry (later General Lord) Rawlinson, who was befriended by Lady Roberts and her daughters, similarly noted in August 1888 that she 'is the most impossible person to get on with for those to whom she takes a dislike'. She could not hide her prejudices 'and if she hears a story (and there are many about) relating to anyone she dislikes, whether it be true or not, she refuses to ask them to the house and ignores them entirely'.[88] In September 1888, Rawlinson wrote, 'I can only regret that Lady R. has any knowledge of the official patronage, which should be solely and entirely under Sir F ['s] own thumb.'[89]

Later, in South Africa in November 1900, Rawlinson noted that Roberts 'will not subordinate his personal convenience and desires to the public interest. It has always been the same.' Rawlinson saw this as the reason Lady Roberts had arrived in South Africa with her daughters 'and all through his career it has been this inclination which has kept Lady R and the family in close touch behind him and has so militated against his own great name and her individual popularity'.[90]

There is an indication of Nora's influence, too, in the memoirs of General Sir Ian Hamilton when he remarked of Roberts's journey to Burma in 1886 that he 'would not enter Mandalay; the place was taboo to him, or perhaps Lady Roberts had tabooed it'.[91] Hamilton's own marriage to Jean Muir, a wealthy woman with literary and artistic tastes, was initially opposed by Nora. Hamilton declined to postpone the marriage as

Roberts requested in August 1886, but he then had to accompany Roberts to Burma. Jean wrote that Hamilton

> begs me to be nice to Lady Bobs as he says so much depends on this and says: 'the best way to do this is to meet her advances more than half way.' However, she does not seem likely to make any, and if she does I can't meet her more than half way. As well ask me to jump over the moon; she terrifies me. But if I decide to marry Major H. she will just have to lump it . . .'[92]

Ian and Jean were finally married in February 1887. Jean Hamilton became an accomplished hostess and worked assiduously to cultivate the well-connected on Hamilton's behalf as he rose in rank and influence after the South African War.

When there seemed some possibility of Roberts being offered the Viceroyalty in 1893, 'Ladyship' was adamant that Roberts should not return to India. As Hamilton wrote, 'She is staunch as usual, but I can see that she would rather we did not return to India.'[93] In South Africa, as the Queen rightly surmised, there was much talk of 'petticoat government' in the headquarters at Pretoria. Roberts's aide-de-camp, Lord Kerry, Lansdowne's son, even suggested that the conversion of the commander-in-chief to a much tougher line towards Boer women and children owed most to the presence of Lady Roberts.[94] Himself no stranger to the importance of female influence, Douglas Haig complained to his sister when he believed he was likely to be passed over for the command of the Aldershot cavalry brigade in September 1902, 'so no doubt some of Roberts' pals (or? Lady R's pals) have been chosen . . .'. Such influence continued when Roberts became C-in-C at home.

In this context, the destruction of the correspondence that passed between Roberts and his wife by Roberts's biographer David James in 1954 is perhaps suggestive of a desire to conceal the extent to which she influenced him.[95] Few of Nora's letters survive, but it is interesting to compare those that do with the correspondence of Loo Wolseley. While recounting to her husband those events at home of immediate professional concern to him, Loo's letters are also often detailed in their reportage of social and domestic events. She also enjoyed an extensive correspondence with literary and artistic figures far removed from military affairs. By contrast, the one collection of Lady Roberts's letters so far located – those received between 1879 and 1884 by Roberts's former ADC, Melgund – are detailed discussions of military matters, as if Nora was acting as her husband's military secretary.[96] They certainly suggest that she stepped well beyond any notion of separate spheres, while the circumstantial evidence is that there was little subordination in her relationship with her husband.

In defence of Lady Roberts, Sir Charles Nairne recalled in 1896 that when Lieutenant General David Macfarlan had been inspector general of artillery in India, he had not got on with Roberts because he would

> insist on resenting what he called Lady R's interference. This need not have troubled him, for in reality it did not affect the affairs of the Army as her enemies chose to think it did, if indeed it ever deserved the name of interference at all. She occasionally came into the room while the Chief was at work, but it was generally to borrow a pencil or ask Sir F. R. for some trifle that he knew & she did not. Of course, it was wrong but why carp at a woman for not being always right as to official etiquette.[97]

Nora was not unusual or unique in her attempted role, and had much in common with many aristocratic and middle-class women in civilian life and especially politics. She, her husband and children formed a close-knit family, but despite the loss of four of their six children, three in infancy and their son, Freddy, in the Battle of Colenso in 1899 at the age of 27, Nora remained a force to be reckoned with despite her personal tragedies. Roberts died while visiting the Indian Corps in Flanders in November 1914. Nora died in 1920.

The wives of leading soldiers often did play significant roles behind the scenes in the late Victorian army. In so doing, they were not necessarily confined by any perception of separate private and public spheres. More information may still come to light, but it is also clear that the incorporation of women in the army through marriage neither automatically implied their subordination nor constrained their ambition.

Chapter 6

Memory and Reputation: Dorothy Haig

In September 1902 Lieutenant Colonel Douglas Haig believed he was likely to be passed over for the command of the Aldershot cavalry brigade. Haig complained to his sister, 'so no doubt some of Roberts' pals (or? Lady R's pals) have been chosen . . .'[1] Haig may have suspected Lady Roberts, but he himself was no stranger to the importance of female influence. His mother, Rachel, and his sister, Henrietta, had already shaped his character and career. Following his mother's death, Haig wrote almost daily to Henrietta until his marriage. Paradoxically, Haig appeared utterly disdainful of women although, a little like Wellington, he respected those who were serious-minded.[2] In the Hon. Dorothy Maud Vivian, also known as Doris, Haig found a woman who not only substantially enhanced his own impressive social connections, but also one who proved a loving and supportive partner. It was a faithful and loving relationship over the years until Douglas's death at the age of 67 in 1928. Even after his death, Dorothy did everything in her power to promote his qualities both as a military leader (often in opposition to popular opinion) and as a family man.

Dorothy was a 26-year-old maid of honour to Queen Alexandra when she first met Douglas. She had been placed opposite him at a dinner during a weekend party for Ascot Week at Windsor Castle in May 1905. Twin daughter of the 3rd Lord Vivian, Dorothy had been born on 8 July 1879. Douglas was on home leave from his appointment as Inspector General of Cavalry in India. Although Haig had commanded the regiment in which Dorothy's brother, the 4th Lord Vivian, served, she had not previously met him. Indeed, her brother had laughed when Dorothy had asked to be introduced to Douglas at a polo match earlier, for Douglas had the reputation of 'rather a women-hater'.[3] This appears, however, to have been somewhat exaggerated.[4] A few days later, they were formally introduced and it was arranged, fairly haphazardly, that they should play golf together, the opposing partners being the Duke of Devonshire and another lady. Their conversation on this occasion was intermittent and of a general nature. Douglas kept pulling out and looking at his watch. Dorothy assumed he was finding time with her tedious, but Douglas told her that the watch had been given to him by his mother to give to his future wife.

They arranged to play again the next day before breakfast, but on arrival Douglas paid off the caddies, saying he no longer wished to play. In the awkward silence that followed they looked for a seat, but finding none Douglas 'blurted out, "I must propose to you standing!"'[5] Dorothy accepted him, and less than four months later, on 11 July 1905, they were married at the Private Chapel in Buckingham Palace, at the request of the Queen. The chapel had never previously been used for a non-royal wedding. The King was apparently amused by the courtship, asking Haig what he meant 'coming to my house and trying to take away one of the Queen's best Maids of Honour'. He also told Dorothy she should not interfere with the work of 'my best and most capable General'.[6] Initially Lady Vivian declined to see Haig but he persisted and, with the assistance of a letter from Queen Alexandra, permission for the marriage was granted.

The brevity of their acquaintance prior to their marriage has often raised questions, although the age gap of eighteen years was not unusual among the middle classes in general and army officers particularly. Haig's father had been nineteen years older than his wife, and many of Haig's contemporaries married in their forties and fifties. It has often been suggested that Haig was motivated by Dorothy's position and close connection to the Queen, but he already had royal connections. His sister, Henrietta, had been close to the King when he was Prince of Wales. Haig had visited Sandringham as early as 1898 and he had become ADC to the King in 1902. In part the rumours seem to have come about from his reply to a friend who had commented on the suddenness and the brevity of their engagement. Haig replied 'Why not? I have often made up my mind on more important matters than that of my own marriage in much less time.'[7] Whatever he really felt, Dorothy seemed unaffected by the gossips, and Haig had acquired a wife, generally thought vital for an officer of his rank. His choice enhanced his position both socially and career-wise.

Dorothy's memoir of Douglas, *The Man I Knew*, was published in 1936. Through Dorothy's stories, we see her both as one extremely cosseted, and yet displaying stamina under duress. She had a knack, most useful to Douglas, of not being overwhelmed with nerves when meeting notably 'difficult' men in social situations. On one occasion, Douglas had warned Dorothy that Lord Kitchener was 'not at his best with women', but Dorothy was blessed with a natural charm that neither shrank from nor fawned over powerful individuals. Dorothy recalls 'I was rather flattered that a few days before we left, Lord Kitchener asked me to push about his furniture in the living room because he felt it wanted a feminine hand.'[8] Dorothy's main concern in this instance was that she was afraid she might break a piece of Kitchener's valuable collection of Oriental porcelain.

Douglas had been reluctant to return to India after his marriage. He would have preferred to gain appointment as Director of Staff Duties at the War Office, but he and Dorothy established their new married life in India. Of Douglas – his first time there as a married man – Dorothy wrote candidly, 'I want to point out here Douglas's extraordinary patience in dining out every night and staying up late at dances to please me. As a bachelor he had rarely dined out (which he did not mention to me, but I heard so from others), and certainly he did not go near balls, especially as he could not dance.'[9] She did break this cycle of behaviour after noticing him, 'in the early hours of one morning seeing him sitting in his red uniform and hiding so well his boredom'. From then on, she wrote, 'I feel rather proud that I avoided staying late again, pretending that I was sick of meeting the same people night after night.'[10] She did admit to having 'a good fling when alone', and she comes over as being genuinely caring in her self-sacrifice in this matter. She praised, as always, her husband's outstanding unselfishness, to the point of her 'not always fully realising how much he was sacrificing himself for me then and always and afterwards for his children'.[11] They wrote to each other most days, she sometimes twice or three times in one day.

There were quite a number of stories that Dorothy related throughout her book which had nothing whatsoever to do with her husband, but focused instead on trivia concerning the niceties of getting dressed, arranging hair and suchlike. This added a sour note to the reviewers of her book, who were seeking more depth. An example, which may have caused poor Douglas to turn in his grave, was her tribute to him 'for the way he helped me to dress at Simla. He would allow time, after dressing himself, to fasten the devilish hooks. At first he was rather clumsy and fumbled a bit, but after a few days he soon mastered the job.'[12] She repeatedly mentioned comments made by others to Douglas concerning her own fine qualities. During his time at the War Office, to which Haig returned as Director of Military Training in 1906, when they were dining with the Royal Family, she recalled that, 'Douglas was delighted because the Queen remarked to him at dinner that my hair was well turned out.'[13] Dorothy was very proud of her closeness with Queen Alexandra, and wrote of it many times. She included a press cutting from the time of the birth of their first child, Alexandra, in March 1907. It referred to her as the Queen's favourite maid of honour, and that the Queen showed 'her great interest in Mrs Haig, by being sponsor to her first child'.[14] The King had certainly pressed for Haig to be brought back to the War Office, but there is no evidence that the friendship between the Royal Family and Dorothy had any bearing on this matter

At times, she became weary of his daily, lengthy meetings at the War Office. She complained that when friends came to dine with them from the War Office, 'they were too fond of discussing after dinner, the work they had been doing during the day'. She recalled teasing Douglas and saying that 'he ought to leave shop talk alone'. She admitted that as she was not able to contribute to their discussions she often fell asleep in a chair. She was peeved to find that when she awoke, usually after midnight, 'none had noticed, being so absorbed in what they were talking about'.[15] She did have genuine concerns about Douglas's health, but at times she appeared to be more upset about being ignored rather than understanding the world as it was then, with 'men's work' taking absolute precedence over small talk with 'mere' women.

Dorothy was certainly able to be relied upon to fulfil her role as dutiful wife when the need arose, and Douglas took it for granted that she would complete the domestic tasks necessitated by their frequent changes of residence. When they returned to India in 1909 upon Douglas's appointment as Chief of Staff to the Commander-in-Chief, General Sir O'Moore Creagh, Douglas told her that she needed to get their quarters in Calcutta furnished in two days. She undertook the task with energy and enthusiasm, to the extent of haggling in bazaars for bargains. She saw it as a challenge to transform existing fabrics, such as redundant curtains, into sofa and chair covers. She was a wonderful organizer, and wherever they went, she instantly became part of the social groups. 'One was able to get away', she comments 'from the eternal military scene and come across many very interesting people.'[16]

Although Dorothy did not keep Douglas late at dances during this time, she did not let this curb her social enjoyment. She described some occasions as very rowdy, including some kind of dance she characterized as 'imitating the apache'. Many of these high jinks were made more intense by the amount of wine she and her guests drank. 'Pigsticking', where 'ladies ride on young men's backs and use billiard cues as spears', was responsible for an accident which stopped a party. She recalled Douglas being 'astounded' at the magnitude of the bill for the wine. He was said to comment that they must have had enough drink for an army.[17] Dorothy added that the stories of these rowdy occasions did the rounds. Apparently, Douglas was not angry with her, but only laughed.

Dorothy showed remarkable compassion for those less fortunate than herself. A group of her acquaintances showed a keenness for helping with first aid, and Dorothy felt that if they were to maximize their usefulness during wartime, they should try to gain practical experience. She took it upon herself to arrange for them to receive training at a small hospital in Simla. Once the basic skills of bed-making, bandaging and similar had been mastered, Dorothy insisted that they should go to the out-patients department and do dressings, under a hospital doctor's guidance.

On their first day, a man who had been bitten by a snake required the amputation of his swollen and infected finger. Dorothy noted everything down as it happened, but her class gradually drifted away, not having the stomach for it. Her ability to remain unaffected by such gruesome sights made her an asset in a hospital where the resources and staff were extremely stretched. Douglas encouraged his wife to keep on with her medical training and that of other ladies, as nursing arrangements for war were considerably lacking. It did not seem to cross his mind of the risks to her health, and Dorothy was brave to continue, as regular cases admitted were plague, cholera, dysentery, malaria and leprosy. Dorothy's work eventually led to the formation of Voluntary Aid Detachments (VADs) in India.

Both Dorothy and Douglas were delighted with his posting back to England for the Aldershot Command in 1911. On their journey home from India, aboard the SS *Oceania*, Dorothy contracted a severe bout of dysentery, which she put down to sleeping in a damp tent at Delhi. She was not expected to survive, but commented later that 'I managed to cheat the doctor that time, as I have done again on more than one occasion'.[18]

When the Haigs left for India, they had left their daughters, Alexandra then aged two and Victoria aged nine months, in the care of Douglas's sister Henrietta. In 1911 Alexandra fell ill and had to have an operation to remove glands, causing Dorothy some distress.[19] It says much about Dorothy that she totally supported her husband in going to India, and accepted the importance of the supportive role of a wife, even if it meant handing over the care of their young family. Upon their return three years later, The Haigs and their daughters were complete strangers to each other. The girls were very quiet on the car journey home, and Dorothy commented to their nurse upon their good behaviour. The nurse replied that they were often very wild, which Dorothy certainly found to be true when she began to care for them, with only the help of their nursery maid. Dorothy looked back on those days with mixed feelings, and by her own admission was 'quite unaccustomed to children, and they were up to every conceivable trick they could think of'.[20] She viewed it more as an ordeal to be endured than a pleasurable re-acquaintance. She was sad that the children refused to kiss her at bedtime for some months, and it brought home to her the disadvantages for families forced by army life to leave their children for most of their young lives. She found their high spirits and disregard for precious and fragile 'knick-knacks' on display around the house hard to deal with, and felt surprised to find herself in situations, which seemed beyond her control.

Douglas remained in command at Aldershot until the outbreak of war in August 1914 when, as expected, he was named to command I Corps in the British Expeditionary Force (BEF). When Douglas left for France in August 1914, he left behind a wife who he was confident he could depend upon for caring for the wives and families at Aldershot. He also told her just before leaving that he had specifically asked the girls 'to be kind to their mummy'. And Douglas reassured her that 'they would be a great comfort to her in the days to come'.[21]

One aspect of Dorothy's wartime experience was to resume her mantle of competent wife, organizing a Red Cross maternity camp where mothers were given excellent care and their offspring could thrive. She didn't take all the credit, praising the colonels' wives in particular, of whom she said 'splendidly faced all their difficulties'.[22] As difficulties in day-to-day living increased and hygiene problems escalated, Dorothy chose to 'pack my two small girls off to North Wales to be under the charge of my twin sister'.[23] She admitted to missing them 'bitterly', but felt it was for the best. This gave Dorothy free rein to serve the war effort and comply with the pledges that Douglas sometimes made on her behalf without consulting her. She never complained, but simply got on with each task, however daunting it seemed. Douglas had promised the Empress Eugénie, widow of Napoleon III of France, who now lived in Farnborough, that Dorothy would organize and run a hospital in the Empress's house. Dorothy did so, and used her ingenuity, never in short supply, by converting one of the bathrooms into an operating theatre. She never left the menial tasks to others; she cleaned the theatre, prepared swabs, ordered stores and paid all the bills. All this, she said, 'was a great help in keeping me from worrying'.[24] Dorothy was amused by King George V's remark to Douglas that he had seen her 'pretending to be a nurse!'

Douglas wrote to Dorothy every day, including pages from his diary. He apologised at one point in August 1914 for the lack of words, due to 'the rapidity with which they were retreating', the BEF having to fall back after its first encounter with the Germans at Mons.[25] In common with a number of leading figures including the Commander-in-Chief of the BEF, Field Marshal Sir John French, and the commander of I Corps, General Sir Horace Smith-Dorrien, Douglas had been asked to correspond either directly with the King or through his private and assistant private secretaries, respectively Lord Stamfordham and Clive Wigram.[26] This was to prove highly significant both in terms of Haig's ability to convey his views to the Palace, but also in terms of Haig's later much-disputed legacy as wartime commander. The diaries, or rather the apparent later addition of some of the comments in the diaries continues to attract attention. Douglas trusted Dorothy to select what was passed to the King, writing to her on 28 April 1915:

> As regards copies of my diary to Wigram – use your own judgment in this end and send him whatever you think necessary, but I hope you will limit these extracts to past events and not future plans. With this exception, send him whatever you like – and if there is anything about which he wishes information, of course tell him.[27]

At one point, Wigram asked for the diary to be forwarded directly to him, and only sent to Dorothy at a later time. She wrote to Douglas of this, as she felt that it would impede him in saying what he truly felt was happening. Douglas replied immediately that he would send separate dictated reports to the King, but that he would continue to send the diaries, which were written for her alone.[28] The nature of much of what Douglas wrote to her was highly sensitive, including maps he had marked so that she could follow the movements of I Corps, instructing her to keep all maps and diaries secret. She recalled that he 'continually thanked her for taking such trouble over his "stupid opinions and stories"',[29] and she became especially possessive of the diaries in the certainty that they had indeed been intended for her alone.

Dorothy generally got her own way, even over the wishes of the King, who had asked Douglas to see him in London as a matter of urgency when he was on a brief home leave in March 1915. She replied, insisting that Douglas stayed a few days more at Folkestone, as he had been exhausted. She received a reply from the King, saying that he quite understood. Dorothy had influence in Douglas's life from the highest order to the most mundane; she knitted all his ties, insisting that he wore no others.

At the time of the Battle of Loos in September 1915, Dorothy gave up her hospital work to devote time to family needs. Due to increasing Zeppelin raids on London, once again she took her children to Wales. This gave her more time to devote to war work. During the day she worked with severely-injured troops at St Dunstan's, and in the evenings she helped with the cooking at a hut in Victoria Station for officers returning from the Front. This work inspired her to champion the needs and problems that faced many returning from battle. She was tireless in her efforts both physically and in fundraising to ensure continuing assistance for the disabled. Her status as the wife of Douglas Haig gave her confidence to approach those in high office and other wealthy business people for large donations for what was to become the Disabled Officers' Fund.

With Haig once more on a brief home leave in November 1915, they were invited to lunch with the Prime Minister, Herbert Asquith. Dorothy recalled that Douglas was flustered by the barrage of questions from the frighteningly astute Margot Asquith. He reacted by simply 'leaving the questions unanswered, casting many a worried look across the table' to her, knowing that she could reply satisfactorily due to her knowledge of his diaries.[30] Haig was notoriously inarticulate, particularly in the company of politicians, and as a couple he and Dorothy complemented each other very well. Whenever Douglas returned from difficult and dreadful situations, Dorothy took great pains to provide as stress-free a sanctuary as possible in which Douglas could recover. She had the knack of making anywhere home for him, where they could spend quiet evenings together away from the angst of all that leading a country at war brings with it. Their closeness was such that Dorothy wrote that Douglas 'had many times commented before how, just as he had been thinking of something, I had written to him on that particular subject'.[31] She was also excellent at sustaining good feeling between her husband and those under his command, and she never overlooked the 'servant class'. At Christmas 1916, she sent a present to everyone in the headquarters. She included her husband, his ADCs and a soldier-servant in wrapping these gifts on Christmas Eve.[32]

Douglas succeeded to the command of the BEF on 19 December 1915. He was now to preside over the controversial and increasingly costly attempts to break through the German defences on the Western Front, principally the Somme offensive of July to November 1916 and the Third Ypres or Passchendaele offensive of August to November 1917.[33] Douglas wrote to Dorothy during the Somme campaign that he was looking forward to the quiet years in the future that he would spend with her 'far away from all the bustle and jealousies of the "*Important*"'. He reflected on 'the quiet home we will have together and how we would live our own lives with the children and find out for ourselves how the nursery governess was so successful in making them so extraordinarily good'.[34] They both felt that they had missed out on family life, perhaps Douglas more so than Dorothy who always seemed to flourish in the absence of her children, devoting herself to the benefit of others.

Douglas was rarely distant and aloof with his wife, as many in similar positions chose to be. He respected her as an equal in intelligence, ahead of his time in many ways, and benefitted greatly from doing so. Dorothy was wise enough to know her acceptable limits and wrote that, although he totally confided in her, 'he never tolerated any interference by me in military matters'.[35] She found this to be true when she was asked to raise a sensitive question, regarding the future of Douglas's head of military intelligence, Brigadier General John Charteris, in her letters to him. With trepidation, she did what she had been asked to do, but recalled that 'Douglas completely ignored it and made no reference to it whatsoever'.[36] Dorothy had never liked Charteris, who had become Douglas's assistant military secretary in India. Charteris was superficially clever and certainly more lucid than Douglas in spoken and written word. Dorothy, however, thought him vulgar and 'dirty'.[37] She was certainly more perceptive than Douglas when it came to Charteris, whose wildly optimistic intelligence reports fed Douglas's ever more certain belief that one more attack would crack the

German will to resist. It was only after the disasters of Passchendaele that Douglas was finally forced to dispense with Charteris's dubious services.

In the summer of 1917 Dorothy, somewhat amused to find herself viewed as an expert on hospital management, was invited to go to Paris to visit the hospitals. Despite being keen to accept this opportunity, Dorothy sensed that Douglas, although he did not say so, was afraid that such a visit might set a precedent for women to visit the Front, which he had no wish to encourage. Dorothy chose not to go.

Douglas was always able to confide in his wife over the triumphs and disasters he experienced. She was a buffer for his hurts and disappointments, especially the criticisms he received from David Lloyd George over strategies employed. Succeeding Kitchener as Secretary of State for War in June 1916, Lloyd George was already critical of the growing list of casualties and what he saw as the obsession of Douglas and the Chief of the Imperial General Staff, Sir William Robertson, with the war on the Western Front. Succeeding the ineffective Asquith as Prime Minister in December 1916, Lloyd George was determined to replace Douglas if he could, or find some means of effecting his resignation. Lloyd George's difficulty was that, with the Liberals split over the ousting of Asquith, he was highly dependent upon the Conservatives who supported Douglas's conduct of the war. Douglas confided to Dorothy that if dismissed he 'would be perfectly happy to come to me in our new home and help me bring up our children' although this seems somewhat unlikely.[38]

Dorothy prided herself on developing antennae for those opposed to Douglas. Yet, it could be argued that, because she hated the idea of Douglas pandering to the public, she encouraged his myopic attitude towards the press. In that way she was less helpful despite her overall contribution to his success, as he did not see the need to explain the increasing casualty bill.[39] One of Lloyd George's ploys was to try and force Douglas to resign by placing the BEF under the overall command of the French general, Robert Nivelle, in the spring of 1917. Douglas was able to outflank Lloyd George with the assistance of the King and it was negotiated that the BEF would only come under French control for the forthcoming operation, but with Douglas having full right of appeal to London. A French officer brought the final agreement to Douglas when he was in the London flat Dorothy had taken. She saw 'hatred written clearly over the horrible man's face'.[40] In the event, Douglas's position was strengthened by the episode, not least when the Nivelle offensive failed and much of the French army mutinied.

Douglas was able to justify his plans for the Passchendaele offensive by emphasising the need to take on the main burden to enable the French to recover. There were those who supported Douglas against Lloyd George. One was the Secretary of State for War, Lord Derby, who suggested he should recommend a peerage. Douglas felt the Field Marshal's rank granted him in January 1917 sufficient, remarking that if he accepted he and Dorothy 'would probably start living beyond our means and end in the bankruptcy court'.[41]

According to Dorothy, Douglas 'intended to completely ignore Lloyd George's attacks on his leadership, as he was sure the people at home would not be influenced by such incorrect statements'.[42] As the Passchendaele offensive continued, Dorothy said that 'Douglas assured me that all the War Cabinet, with the exception of the Prime Minister, were confident of our ultimate success'. She continued, 'The fact that he knew I whole-heartedly agreed with his intentions, helped him to carry on with a perfectly easy conscience, under conditions made more difficult by the Prime Minister's attacks on the army'.[43] She finished, 'Anxiety about the weather seemed to trouble Douglas really more than what politicians said about him!'[44]

When it was demanded that the British length of the Western Front be substantially increased, Haig, although reluctant to put his job on the line by resisting this proposal, given the depleted state of the army, wrote to her, 'As far as I am concerned the Versailles Conference went off quite well, but don't let that trouble your pretty little head. The machinery is so big and clumsy it will take some time before it can work fast enough to trouble me. So I don't mean to be influenced by it against my better conscience.'[45]

All through the most difficult of times Douglas was able to offload to Dorothy his worries and painful decisions. The death of Haig's first wartime chief of staff, Johnnie Gough, from a sniper's bullet on 22 February 1915 deeply affected Douglas. His letters to Dorothy often seem to have been a sounding board for his own feelings, and in this case he may have been attempting to brush off guilt that accompanied the fact that he had advised Gough to take command of a new division at home. Johnnie had been hit while taking leave of his old battalion in the front line. Haig wrote to Dorothy that at Gough's funeral, Dorothea Gough 'bore up wonderfully, but I did not like to intrude upon her grief, so I did not speak to her'. He told Gough's old comrade, Reginald Stephens that he 'felt like a murderer'.[46] This was unusual behaviour from Douglas, and the fact that he was able to express his feelings to his wife must have been a great comfort to him, as he knew she would never sit in judgment. It was noted by those around him that Douglas was more affected by Gough's death than any other and that it was the only time during the war when Douglas allowed any personal incident to interrupt his normal routine.

Douglas's letters to Dorothy regarding the war and other campaigns were always a mix of the military detail and personal reflections. It is through his closeness and heart searching in corresponding with his beloved wife that history has gained surprising knowledge of the inner man. His feelings changed in the extreme from one day to the next. One day – as in the case of the offensive at Neuve Chapelle in March 1915 – he would be optimistic, 'Enemy quite surprised – so hope for large results', and the next that, although French had been delighted with progress, 'Personally I am disappointed we did not get further'.[47]

Dorothy was a perpetual source of support. She was very much more involved in his work life than many wives, whose roles were completely devoted to domestic matters. Their devotion was not a secret and it was noted that when Douglas was able to take a short break on one occasion in December 1916, unusually the trip 'was so thoroughly occupied with business, he did not even see Lady Haig!'[48] Douglas would write to her of some of the more trivial and humorous aspects of the war, often confiding in her with regards to the effect of a little too much alcohol on some of the major players in government, commenting in September 1916 on Lloyd George's capacity for drink.[49]

With a major German offensive expected on the Western Front in the spring of 1918, following the German success in knocking Russia out of the war, Dorothy was expecting again. Understandably, Douglas could not be with his wife at the time of the birth, but felt the need to write Dorothy a 'charming letter, explaining all this, and saying he knew I would understand'. He managed to visit his wife at their newly acquired home at Kingston Hill twice during this period prior to the birth of the child. This included accompanying her on a 45-minute walk in the park, presumably to hasten the onset of labour, in which it did not succeed. When she eventually delivered a healthy baby boy, George, on 15 March 1918 Douglas is said to have given way to one of his rare displays of emotion, including kissing the medical officer.[50]

A constant factor in their marriage appeared to be their shared passion for golf, a game that originally forged their attraction to each other. The traumas and tragedies of the war were punctuated by their disappointment over the ground being too hard or wet for them to get in as many rounds as possible during periods of leave. For them to have this shared interest temporarily enabled them to focus on something other than reality. One thing that also united husband and wife was a shared concern for each other's health. Douglas was always concerned over Dorothy's welfare and comfort, as he commented in a letter in November 1926 to his friend and former wartime medical office, 'Micky' Ryan: 'I was delighted to see so much improvement in my wife's condition y'day [*sic*] . . . you are a wonderful fellow.'[51] Dorothy did suffer from poor health on many occasions, but she was able to bear it with such cheerful temperament that it endeared her to Douglas, rather than becoming burdensome to him. She was particularly vulnerable to diseases and conditions which prevailed whilst accompanying Haig on overseas postings, and the fragility of her health at times had influenced Haig's decisions over application for, or acceptance of, appointments before the war.

Dorothy had a regular mutual correspondence with Ryan, to whom she wrote in December 1915 of her 'deep debt of gratitude for looking after Douglas during the "retreat" and after. This has enabled him to stand the strain.'[52] Dorothy fussed and fretted about Douglas's health, particularly his mental condition. On 29 March 1918 she wrote to Ryan that would he 'be an angel and let me know when you have seen Douglas what you candidly think of him after all this strain'.[53] In similar vein, Douglas was always worried about Dorothy's ability to cope in his absence, and her need of support. In 1918 Douglas to wrote to his wife of Ryan, when Dorothy was pregnant that it 'gave him a great feeling of confidence that he is in the house with you and able to help you in any way required. I am sure you will find him a great comfort.'[54]

With her approaching confinement in February 1918, Douglas reported to Dorothy that Ryan had been 'loud in his delight at seeing you so fit and free from nerves'.[55] He also comforted her that he would bring home some meat with him. Dorothy had become accustomed to being able to call on Ryan for help, but Ryan's wife never showed signs of resentment. In fact, she too was close to Dorothy, sending her special foods such as woodcock when they became available. In March 1918 Dorothy wrote to her that she was reluctant to have her imminent confinement overseen by another doctor: 'I am going to scream for the chloroform and your husband!'[56]

Dorothy and Douglas also shared a belief in God. Haig's mother and sister had equally been interested in religion. Rachel Haig was especially devout while Henrietta dabbled in spiritualism. Douglas, too, attended some of his sister's séances although there is no evidence that he did so after 1908.[57] The sessions had invariably predicted Douglas's future greatness. Douglas's letters to Dorothy presented their shared fervent belief in an unspecified and controlling force beyond themselves. As Douglas wrote to her in December 1915 after taking command of the BEF, 'all seem to expect success as the result of my arrival, and somehow give me the idea that I am meant to win by some Superior power. As you know, I feel ones best can go but a short way without help from above.'[58] On 30 June 1916, on the eve of the start of the Somme offensive, Douglas wrote of their common belief that 'whether or not we are successful lies in the Power above . . . so I am easy in my mind and ready to do my best tomorrow whatever happens'.[59] As Douglas again wrote in April 1917, Dorothy could 'rest assured that I am not likely to forget to whom belongs the honour and the glory for all our good work and success'.[60] Predictably, after the success of the British offensive at Amiens on 8 August 1918 Douglas wrote of the Divine Power that 'all the honour must be his'.[61]

Amiens was the first British counter-attack after the failure of the German Spring Offensives. The 'Hundred Days' from 8 August to 11 November 1918 proved a stunning series of victories, although the extent to which Douglas himself was responsible for victory remains hotly debated.[62] On 11 November 1918 Douglas wrote to Dorothy that at the forefront of his thankful heart, after God, came Dorothy: 'Thank you too for being such a good true little wife to me through these long black days since I left you at Aldershot in August 1914.'[63] For her part, Dorothy recorded, 'It was difficult to realise that the war was at an end, or to rejoice when there were so many sorrowing hearts.'[64]

That day, she attended a meeting in connection with the plan for disabled officers' clubs. Her heart was turned towards the many injured returners, for whom the war would never truly be over. Douglas wholeheartedly supported her in this. At Dorothy's suggestion he lost no time in arranging for £5,000 to be transferred from army funds in France which he hoped could be a donation rather than a loan. A particular concern was for the plight of commissioned officers who, it seemed, were being left to fend for themselves in desperate situations. At the time there were a number of organizations representing ex-servicemen and, with Dorothy's help, Douglas was to play a major role in drawing out the potential dissension by encouraging unity among these groups. Douglas had returned home with 'a fixed determination to live out his remaining years in the service of the brave men who had saved their country'.[65] He promised 'not only money, but all the energy I may have left after the war is over to help disabled men who have suffered in this war'.[66] While the Officers' Association remained technically separate from the organizations representing other ranks, all were effectively merged in the British Legion in July 1921.[67] The Earl Haig Fund – Douglas was created Earl Haig in January 1921 – was established in 1921 to care for ex-servicemen. Lady Haig's Poppy Factory was then established in Edinburgh in 1926.

Upon his being offered a peerage, Dorothy supported Douglas's decision to request that any reward for himself would not be acceptable to him until the Prime Minister had arranged for suitable allowances for not only the disabled, but all ranks of the armies. Many wives would have not been so keen to forgo such honours bestowed upon their husbands, but Dorothy and Douglas shared their compassion for those less fortunate than themselves. This caused difficulties in the honours being awarded to Admiral Beatty, who had accepted without condition, as they could not give him the honour unless Douglas accepted too. This situation did not alter the Haigs' decision to insist first that adequate provision be provided for those in need. Both she and Douglas were resolute that they only wanted sufficient pension to live for the rest of their lives comfortably without monetary anxieties.

There was still much ill-feeling between Lloyd George and Haig, especially concerning the type of welcome-home celebration for those in command. Dorothy wrote that Douglas had been treated by Lloyd George over this matter in a way that was 'surely difficult to imagine a greater insult'. Douglas was reported to have said that 'he would rather go off in a taxi from the station with Dorothy'.[68] With all this going on Dorothy had the added worry of the influenza pandemic which touched her home. She recalled being 'rather upset' at the death of her housemaid. She commented 'I was rather concerned about Douglas's comfort being interfered with. Influenza had depleted my staff and I found it impossible to replace them.'[69] She lost her altruism when it inconvenienced her, and the ability to see her own employees as suffering human beings seemed to have temporarily escaped her. Douglas, however, 'would not allow her to worry over the matter'.[70]

The Haigs' last child, Irene, was born in October 1919, and Dorothy commented that 'in later years she was to prove a great happiness to my husband'.[71] She thought he was reluctant to spoil his son, but unhesitatingly showered affection on their daughters. Dorothy formed a stronger bond with her son, in whom she saw signs of Douglas's unselfish nature. The first flow of her affections had always been for her husband, and she warmed to the child whose nature most resembled his. Their home and family life was undoubtedly happy for them all, and during this time Dorothy continued to support her husband in his post-war activities. Douglas succeeded French as Commander-in-Chief of Home Forces in

July 1919 and continued in this post until it was abolished in June 1920. He formally retired in January 1921.

Later that year, Douglas and Dorothy toured South Africa for the inauguration of the British Empire League. During this tour, and the long sea voyage, Dorothy assisted Douglas, not only in a secretarial role, but as a joint partner in preparing Douglas's many speeches, and also putting together maps of the battlefields during the South African War. Golf was not an option, so they became very proficient at deck quoits. She was often the one to break off from the serious side of life, and lighten the stress by suggesting recreational diversions. During the crossing, Douglas received a telephone call from the Mayor of Cape Town. Dorothy noted in passing that this was the first time the phone had been used at sea. She wrote, 'Curiously enough I spoke better on the telephone than Douglas, so he insisted that I should go below and receive the message.'[72] The mayor tasked Dorothy with persuading her husband to appear in uniform upon their arrival. She was respected by all who knew her, or her reputation, and considered competent to act for husband in numerous ways. Douglas, too, knew when she would do a better job than him, and gladly handed over the reins to his wife on many occasions.

Upon their visit to Kimberley, even though the authorities had given up making extravagant presentations to visiting notaries, an exception was made for Dorothy. She was presented with two uncut diamonds. She was warned against taking them away with her because if she had been seen to be in possession of uncut stones, she might 'be imprisoned for I. D. B. [Illicit Diamond Buying]', so she had to hand them back to be cut.[73]

During their visit to Pretoria, unusually in her writings, Dorothy recalled what she referred to as a 'slight disagreement'. She immediately qualified this as a '*very* slight disagreement'.[74] She and Douglas were invited to hunt springbok. She learned that this 'entailed galloping to the spot, driving the springbok in front of one, jumping off and shooting it with a rifle, and I had never used a rifle before'. The prospect terrified her, so she asked their hostess to arrange a visit for her to Victoria Falls, whilst Douglas went on the hunt: 'He was rather annoyed at first', she said, 'but with his usual understanding he let me go.'[75] Douglas had stipulated that she must be back at the farm the day before they left. Upon her return she was horrified to learn that they had kept the best hunt for her, and that they were going that afternoon. Despite her protestations that her hunting habit was packed at the bottom of the case, she was persuaded to go. In true Dorothy style she hastily arranged for the host's son to give her an hour's secret target practice. When the moment arrived, she admitted 'I *felt* I could shoot one'. She took aim, and Douglas called out that she was too far away: 'I paid no attention,' she says, 'and fired and shot my springbok right through the head.'[76] She felt Douglas was very proud, and believed that the shot became part of the local folklore, and the place pointed out to future visitors to the area.

At times Dorothy had little idea that remarks she made might be overheard and result in repercussions. She told of a time when they had been travelling, still in South Africa, and she was without a lady's maid between stops. She always stipulated when asked by the ADC at the larger places they came to, that she must have a maid able to iron well. Upon their approach by train to Bloemfontein, Dorothy was informed that in addition to Douglas inspecting the awaiting guard of honour, that she too would be expected to inspect a guard and make a speech as well. This was not something she was nervous of doing, and she prepared herself well. When she stepped on to the platform she was greeted by a 'squadron' of a hundred ladies' maids who presented her with flat irons. It was done in the best of humours and Dorothy took it in good part, a little perturbed by the fact that this incident may be one that in future telling might define her over and above her more worthy deeds.[77]

During a visit to Canada in 1925, Douglas was due to preside over an important dinner given by the British Empire Service League at the Ritz Carlton Hotel. Douglas was not fit enough to attend and Dorothy was invited to attend in his place, which she did with her usual aptitude for such occasions. She recalled with relish that 'After the dinner we had a splendid dance which lasted until 2.30am'. 'This', she remembered, 'was perhaps foolish, for we were due to leave early next morning by train for Ottawa.'[78] If Douglas had been able to attend the dinner, it is possible that

Dorothy would not have had the opportunity to revisit her ballroom days, which she had selflessly relinquished for Douglas's sake.

She was not always so considerate of his needs, and we see at times the manipulative power of Dorothy over others when she wanted her own way. She was a hard woman to refuse, once she had made up her mind. During their stay in Toronto, she persuaded a Major Shearer to take her over Niagara Falls in an aeroplane, despite the fact that the weather was misty and wet. She wrote of this, 'Had I not used all my persuasiveness, he would have hardly risked taking off.' She added 'this was the first flight over the falls, and we had to fly rather high as the effects of the currents on the machine had not yet been ascertained'.[79] She was a risk-taker indeed, and Shearer was foolhardy in the extreme to bow to her wishes.

Their final home was Bemersyde in Berwickshire, purchased for Haig by the government in 1921, but only occupied by them for the first time in 1924. During this time, Dorothy and Douglas worked together on the war diaries. She retyped them, inserting all the documents he had sent to her for safekeeping. She felt that this work together enabled Douglas to have a purpose in life when his career in the army was over. Their task was complemented as always by recreation, including salmon fishing in the Tweed. As elsewhere in her book, she loved to recall incidents where she was most proud of herself. Here she wrote 'but I think he was proudest of all when I, *who could not fish*, caught the biggest fish of the year from that river'.[80]

Dorothy described Douglas as one who 'to me and our children could not have shown greater love, care and patience'.[81] Sadly for Dorothy, at the time of Douglas's death she was not staying at the same house. Douglas had had a hunting accident, resulting in several broken teeth and a fracture of the jaw, which it was assumed would mend itself. Shortly afterwards, Douglas attended a scout rally in London and stayed with Henrietta. He was found dead of a suspected heart attack during the night of 29 January 1928. It was decided not to inform Dorothy until early the following morning. 'The tragic news,' she says, 'did not reach me until the whole world knew.'[82] In her devastation, she was called upon to answer questions from reporters. It was a 'terrible moment'.

Dorothy had supported Douglas staunchly through the many disappointments and difficulties they had encountered. Douglas concluded his own war diaries, 'Here ends the diary of some of my daily doings during the Great War. It has at times been difficult to write it up, but I always managed to write something for Doris.'[83] The place she held in his heart was immovable from their first meeting until his death.

After Douglas's death Dorothy became immensely protective of his memory and reputation, and the vexed question of the wartime diaries came to the fore. Dorothy and Douglas had already completed some work on the diaries, but Dorothy was concerned that 'passages hurriedly written at the front which may not read well' should be put right.[84] She regarded them as her own property, as she continued to maintain they were written for her and denied the hated Charteris access to them for his memoir, *At GHQ*, in 1931. Haig's executors were keen to commission an authorized biography, but several potential authors were dissuaded by Dorothy's attitude. In March 1933 they chose Duff Cooper, then a junior minister at the War Office and a successful biographer. Duff Cooper insisted on access to all of Douglas's papers, not least the copy of the diaries that had been lodged with the official historian of the war on land, Brigadier General James Edmonds. Dorothy refused and it took the intervention of the Permanent Secretary at the War Office who also happened to be one of the executors, Sir Herbert Creedy, to secure Edmonds's agreement.

Dorothy then announced that she would write the memoir that became *The Man I Knew*. She maintained that Douglas had 'always had at the back of his mind the idea that they [the diaries and letters] would give an account of the true happenings, but he had no anticipation the verdict of history, which has a queer habit of changing and readjusting itself, sometimes fairly, sometimes falsely, as great events recede farther and farther from actuality'.[85] It was left to her, therefore, to 'show the world a great man of action as a simple human being'. She also suggested that prior to Passchendaele, Douglas had asked Dorothy to undertake the writing of his life:

> He always coupled me with any such record and referred it as *our*
> history. He insisted that one day *I* would write it because he was quite
> sure he would be so tired of the whole war and the difficulties that
> were put in his way, that he would be quite unable to write sufficiently
> tolerantly of some of the members of the Government who had made
> his task so irksome.[86]

What Douglas did not realize was that Dorothy's book would be equally
about her. Much of the narrative was wrapped up in her own opinions
on events by expressing them as Douglas's intentions and sentiments.
Dorothy rarely failed to bring herself into the picture.

By putting together the pre-war diaries and papers, which she had
preserved despite Douglas's wish they be destroyed, she was provided
with 'the greatest comfort' after his death because 'they gave me details
of his life before I knew him'. She continued, 'All who knew Douglas will
know of his extraordinary reserve (true to Scots type), and he had told me
very little of what he had done before I married him.'[87] Dorothy hoped to
publish all the letters and diaries, which she painstakingly typed out, but
Duff Cooper's book made it impossible to publish them.

Duff Cooper was horrified by Dorothy's attempt to rush her book out
before his, and took legal action to prevent it. *The Man I Knew*, therefore,
which was considerably shorter than the original manuscript, appeared
in 1936 shortly after the first of Duff Cooper's two volumes. It has been
rather cruelly retitled by some as 'The Man I Didn't Know'.[88] Certainly it
is less revealing of Haig himself than that by his soldier-servant, Sergeant
Thomas Secrett, *Twenty Five Years with Earl Haig*, which was published in
1929.[89] Yet it is immensely valuable for assessing Dorothy's own character.
Dorothy included so much about herself, at times that one feels it should
be retitled 'Chiefly Myself'. When Dorothy died on 17 October 1939, it
was in the knowledge that, despite her efforts, Douglas's reputation had
been badly damaged by the memoirs of the politicians, not least his old
adversary, Lloyd George.

Chapter 7

An Altered Path:
Betty Montgomery

One of Montgomery's seconds-in-command once complained that 'conversation was impossible, you could only talk about the army!'[1] Montgomery was not instinctively sociable, telling his sister Una on one occasion, 'Have a party and I will pay for it and look after you . . . I don't dance, as you know, but I'll look after you.'[2]

Then suddenly in 1925, aged 38, he fell in love with Betty Anderson, a 17-year-old blonde. He was not a natural romantic and this first Betty was clearly not seduced by him tracing out for her his ideas on how to deploy tanks on the sands at St Malo and Dinard in Brittany. Betty Anderson apparently admired his character and ambition, but she did not love him. She turned down his proposal. At the time Montgomery was a major and about to receive accelerated promotion to brevet lieutenant colonel as an instructor at the Staff College, Camberley. Perhaps assuming his promotion would make a difference, Montgomery followed her on a skiing holiday to Switzerland but again she turned him down.

At this same skiing party in Lenk in January 1926 was the 39-year-old Betty Carver, the widow of a Territorial officer killed at Gallipoli in 1915, and the sister of another up-and-coming officer, Patrick 'Percy' Hobart. Betty had two young sons, John and Richard, aged 11 and 13. Montgomery and Betty went their separate ways at the end of the holiday but agreed to keep in touch. They both returned to Lenk in January 1927. There was no engagement, however, and Percy took it upon himself to suggest that Betty get Montgomery to declare his intentions.[3] Montgomery then went on a battlefield tour to Flanders. He finally proposed by the fives court at Charterhouse when he and Betty went to visit her sons' school, but only after Betty said they should stop seeing each other for a while. Montgomery had then said, 'Don't be silly, Betty – I love you'.[4] Betty's youngest son, Richard, was apparently upset, so the engagement was only announced on 25 June. He and Betty were married at Chiswick on 27 July 1927. By all accounts, Betty's family found Montgomery entirely unremarkable.

This love match scenario was so at odds with what one might have expected of Montgomery. One of his maxims was 'You cannot make a good soldier and a good husband.' Upon his engagement to Betty, he was reminded of this, and asked which it was to be.[5] Prematurely middle-aged, Montgomery was decidedly set in his ways and obsessed by his military career. Probably as a result of the ongoing conflict with his mother, Maud, he was practically a misogynist. Maud had exerted such a tyrannical hold over her family, Montgomery being the sixth child, that in later life he refused to acknowledge her in public and refused to attend her funeral in 1949. She had consistently denied him any affection. Ironically, Montgomery would ostensibly inherit some of his mother's worst characteristics.

Betty Carver could not have been more different. She worked as an artist and sculptor from a studio in Chiswick. She had an extensive circle of artistically and literary-minded friends, including the artists Eric Kennington and Augustus John and the novelists Arnold Bennett and Alan Herbert, who was also a close friend of Betty's brother. She admitted to being disorganized and seems to have welcomed Montgomery's controlling nature. Betty told Montgomery's sister, Winsome, 'It's absolute bliss after ten years battling with two small boys and bringing them up . . . But I've had to give up many of my own ideas – he even engages the servants!'[6] It helped also that, once the boys' initial shock wore off, Montgomery got on well with her sons, although his strict organizational regime took time to get used to. Indeed, it was not without courage that Montgomery was prepared to take on two boys.

Montgomery's younger brother, Brian, suggested that Betty had opened Montgomery's eyes to 'a world of people for whom the armed forces counted little, and yet were clearly intelligent, hardworking and highly talented. The memory of this was to stand him in good stead.'[7] Montgomery and Betty's only child, David, was born in August 1928, Montgomery being understandably worried as Betty was then 40. He suggested later that she was never quite as strong afterwards.[8] Betty took Montgomery on holiday to Italy and picnics and bathing parties. His austere past was lightened by a sense of frivolity, which affected his own personality and the way he began to view others. Betty gave him the kind of love and affection he had lacked in his own childhood. In his later memoirs, Montgomery recorded, 'A time of great happiness then began; it had never before seemed possible that such love and affection could exist. We went everywhere, and did everything, together.'[9] The benefits of this marriage were conferred on both sides. Betty's 'softening' effect, as it was often described, made Montgomery a noticeably pleasanter colleague, although once she teasingly suggested he had a 'cruel mouth'.[10]

Following his period at the Staff College, Montgomery commanded the 1st Battalion, The Royal Warwickshire Regiment, which was posted to Palestine in early 1931. Betty followed in June as her son John, by her previous marriage, had been ill. One of Montgomery's officers found Betty 'a charming person'. She was 'full of fun and a lively person to talk to, with a great deal of humour. She often poked fun at Monty – I'm sure they were a devoted couple.'[11] The battalion was posted to India in January 1934, but Montgomery was then appointed chief instructor to the Indian Army's Staff College at Quetta in in June. Long freed of her earlier financial constraints as a widow, Betty was an accomplished hostess. One of the student officers recalled,

> Both she and Monty shared a keen sense of humour and loved pulling one another's legs. They were good and generous hosts, and I was asked to join their dinner parties on several occasions. At one of these, just before a week's spell in camp on outdoor exercises, at the end of dinner, she said: 'Ladies, do come with me and we'll discuss what we are going to do whilst Monty and the men go away to camp to play soldiers.' Monty loved it. They were devoted to one another and didn't mind showing it.[12]

Betty loved dancing until the early hours, and although he rarely accompanied her, Montgomery was pleased to indulge her passion. Another student testified later that there 'was a lightness to the house, and a great deal of amusing chit-chat, gossip and talk quite apart from military discussion'.[13]

In 1937 Betty returned early to England with mild laryngitis. Montgomery followed her at the end of his tenure at Quetta in May. He had two months' leave due him before taking command of the 9th Brigade at Portsmouth and they toured the Lake District. Montgomery became aware that, while Betty remained cheerful and happy, she 'seemed to be weaker than formerly and easily got tired'.[14] Back from the Lake District, Betty took David to Burnham-in-Sea. She was then stung on the foot by an insect, the nature of which was never determined. As Montgomery put it in his memoirs, 'That night her leg began to swell and became painful: a doctor was called and he put her at once into a local Cottage hospital, and sent for me.'[15]

Montgomery, now in command of the 9th Brigade, was due to participate in manoeuvres on Salisbury Plain. He believed that his duty was with his troops over and above domestic problems. In his defence, he was probably not aware of the gravity of Betty's condition, which was worsening by the hour. However, there were many who believed his immediate return to her bedside could have prompted better care, particularly if she had been moved to a larger hospital, where improved resources and a greater range of skills could have been employed.

Betty had very few visitors, her most regular being Jocelyn Tweedie, the fiancée of her son, John Carver. She used to bring David with her, and was shocked by the poor level of care Betty, in such pain, was receiving. Jocelyn assumed that Montgomery did not believe the illness 'was anything much'.[16] Inexplicably, after a short visit, Monty had requested that Jocelyn did not get in touch with anyone about Betty's illness, and he did not take any initiative to find a specialist. Eventually Betty's cousin, Katie Hobart, came over from Ireland, and wrote to Betty's sons of the deterioration of their mother's condition. By the time Monty had managed to arrange a transfer for Betty to Plymouth, she was too frail to be moved. 'Monty,'

Katie wrote, 'has still to learn that in serious illness things do not work out according to plan like ordering an advance at dawn!'[17]

Six days later Katie wrote to Jocelyn that Betty's condition had worsened considerably, her lungs now affected by the septicaemia. In an attempt to curb the spread of poison, her leg was amputated. Pneumonia then set in. Monty in blind optimism began to prepare their new army quarters for an invalid. This was not to be, and on 19 October 1937, Betty died in his arms as he read to her Psalm 23.

As Betty's life was ebbing away, and after her death, Monty's actions, particularly those concerning young David, bordered on cruelty, which even the depths of grief cannot justify. He would not allow Betty's sons to fly home from India – both had been commissioned in the Royal Engineers – and would not allow David either to come and see his mother in her last days or to attend the funeral. The funeral was attended by Montgomery, his brigade-major, his staff captain and his driver. He broke down at the graveside, writing to his stepson John, 'I kissed her dear face for the last time just before the lid was put on.'[18] Later, he wrote of David, 'I could not bring myself to let him see her suffering . . . after the funeral, I went to his school and told him myself. Perhaps I was wrong, but I did what I thought was right.'[19] He also refused all offers of help to look after David from friends and family alike, saying 'I prefer to look after him myself'.[20]

Monty's desolation after the death of his beloved wife altered the life of his young son from one of a loving family, to that of being completely cut off from anything even close to love. From that time onwards, there was what Jocelyn characterized as a 'frightful atmosphere of gloom' about Montgomery.[21] It permeated his life to the extent that he could not bear the company of friends or family. In his memoirs he wrote,

> I was utterly defeated. I began to search my mind for anything I had done wrong, that I should have been dealt such a shattering blow. I could not understand it; my soul cried out in anguish against this apparent injustice. I seemed to be surrounded by utter darkness; all the spirit was knocked out of me. I had no one to love except David and he was away at school.[22]

It has to be said, however, that Montgomery seemed incapable of recognizing the hurt he was causing to David. Edgar 'Bill' Williams, who became Montgomery's chief intelligence officer in Eighth Army, was of the opinion that Monty 'treated David terribly – it broke our hearts to see it'.[23] He spurned what would have been the offer of a good and loving home for David, from his sister Winsome, and gave orders in military style that David was never to be allowed contact with any members of his family. David was passed around like an unwanted parcel, from school to school and a variety of children's holiday homes. During the war, David lived with the family of the headmaster of his preparatory school, whom Montgomery appointed as David's guardian. It was only in 1948 that David moved to Montgomery's new home at Isington Mill near Alton in Hampshire. To his credit, in co-operating on a book on his father with the author, Alistair Horne, David suggested in 1994 that he had never felt deprived himself despite his odd upbringing.[24]

Montgomery had to all intents and purposes learned nothing from the misery of his own mother's lack of affection for him. Perhaps this led to a lifelong inability to open up to his contemporaries. He appeared to have required a monopoly on the grief that beset him following Betty's death. Many years later the military theorist and writer Basil Liddell Hart made some criticism of Montgomery's treatment of Betty in her last days, and also suggested Montgomery had been a bully towards her as to everyone else. Angrily, Montgomery said, 'Never mention her name again'.[25]

Most of the influence of those military wives so far studied has been informed by their lives rather than their deaths. In this case, Betty was unique. Her time as Monty's wife greatly improved the quality of his life, and his character had begun to mellow. In an imagined future with Betty at his side to 'tease him and mollify him',[26] is it possible that he would have developed into a more amenable, less arrogant character? The question also might be asked that, if he had not tragically lost the love of his life, who gave him what he had never experienced – unconditional love and belief in himself – would he have avoided the characteristics that so alienated subordinates and superiors alike: egotism, bombastic self-publicity, arrogance, abrasiveness, belief in his own infallibility, and the disparagement of perceived rivals. Indeed, would he have still become as successful a soldier?

He was left severely emotionally damaged by Betty's death, evident in his neglect and lack of compassion for his son and the rejection of support from others in his family and from friends. He seems not only to have reverted to being much the same in character as he had been before his marriage, but to have added even sharper edges. While Betty was alive he disproved his maxim that he could not be both a good soldier and a good husband. After her death he was eminently *not* a good soldier and a good father. If he had, for one moment, ever seriously considered what Betty would have wished for David after her death, surely he could not have imagined that his actions would have helped her to lie easy in her grave.

Once more, Montgomery dedicated himself wholly to his profession. When war was declared in September 1939 Alan Herbert remarked to his wife, 'Well, perhaps it's a good thing this war's begun. Horrible – but it's a chance for Monty to recover. At last he's got a real job to do.'[27]

Conclusion

To make a generalization by way of concluding these studies of the wives of famous generals would be extremely difficult, the only common factor being that all of them in their own ways, not always positively, did influence the paths of their eminent husbands.

Research for this book has revealed such a spectrum of behaviours and characters among the chosen subjects that there is absolutely no blueprint for any present-day forces wife in the quest for advancement of their spouse. The variety does to some extent reflect the differing eras and their existing attitudes towards women's roles, but character and circumstances emerge as the main players

Some of the women studied here, especially Florentia Sale and Juana Smith, showed courage, endurance and intelligence way beyond the imagination of any action-movie writer. Age did not seem to have been a factor. Frequently on campaign, they could not have foreseen the trials that awaited them, and yet it is fair to say that the actions of Florentia, over 50 years of age, and Juana, a girl of 14, far outshone other wives sharing the same desperate situations, and that they were solely responsible for saving many from death and from giving up hope. They became famous and highly regarded in life, and remembered long after their deaths, eclipsing their male counterparts in every sphere

Some held more sway away from the campaigns, notably Sarah Churchill, whose manipulative skills and royal connections took her husband's career to exceptional heights, but was also responsible for his downfall. Dorothy Haig was a major influence on her husband Douglas, but more because of her loyalty and willingness to be his confidante and 'manager' in their various homes than swaying any military decisions.

The irony of Wellington's Kitty was that by the time his career had flourished, due to the incentive of being eligible to marry her, he no longer loved her, and she had no further influence on his life.

The extraordinary union of Montgomery and Betty Carver tragically became notable for her influence upon him, and his treatment of others, after her untimely death.

As these studies have shown, it appears that in many instances there was more rivalry for the men's career advancement amongst their wives than amongst the men themselves. At times this proved to be more of a major embarrassment or hindrance than a positive influence. A frequent requirement of military wives by soldiers of high rank did appear to be focussed upon their abilities to keep a good house, and to be a decorative figure at a husband's side.

The wives who stood out from the rest were exceptional women, and would have been renowned whatever their life path.

Notes

Abbreviations Used:

APAC = BL, Asia, Pacific and Africa Collections

BL = British Library

CCRO = Cornwall County Record Office

HPL = Hove Public Library

KCL = Campbell Collections, University of KwaZulu-Natal,
    Pietermaritzburg

LHCMA = Liddell Hart Centre for Military Archives

NAM = National Army Museum

RA = Royal Archives

WCRO = Warwickshire County Record Office

Introduction

1. Noel St John Williams, *Judy O'Grady and the Colonel's Lady* (London: Brassey's, 1988).

2. Jennine Hurl-Eamon, *Marriage and the British Army in the Long Eighteenth Century: The Girl I Left Behind Me* (Oxford: Oxford University Press, 2014); Myna Trustram, *Women of the Regiment: Marriage and the Victorian Army* (Cambridge: Cambridge University Press, 1984).

3. For a summary of the literature, see Ian F.W. Beckett, 'Women and Patronage in the Late Victorian Army', *History* 85 (2000), pp. 463–80.

4. Trustram, *Women of the Regiment*, pp. 32, 34.

5. Ibid., pp. 166–7, 188–9, 195–6.

6. Field Marshal Sir Evelyn Wood, *From Midshipman to Field Marshal* 2 vols (London: Methuen & Co., 1906).

7. Field Marshal Lord Roberts, *Forty-One Years in India* 30th [single vol.] edn. (London: Macmillan & Co., 1898).

8. Verity McInnis, *Women of Empire: Nineteenth Century Army Officers' Wives in India and the US West* (Norman, OK: University of Oklahoma Press, 2017).

9. Celia Lee, *Jean, Lady Hamilton, 1861-1941: A Soldier's Wife* (London: Privately printed, 2001); Carol K. Bleser and Lesley J. Gordon (eds), *Intimate Strategies of the Civil War: Military Commanders and Their Wives* (New York: Oxford University Press, 2001).

10. Deborah Kirkwood, 'The Suitable Wife: Preparation for Marriage in London and Rhodesia/Zimbabwe', in Hilary Callan and Shirley Ardener (eds), *The Incorporated Wife* (London: Routledge & Kegan Paul, 1984), pp. 106–19.

11. Frank Prochaska, *Women and Philanthropy in Nineteenth Century England* (Oxford: Oxford University Press, 1980), p. 1.

Chapter 1

1. Frances Harris, *A Passion for Government: The Life of Sarah, Duchess of Marlborough* (Oxford: The Clarendon Press, 1991), p. 57.

2. Winston S. Churchill, *Marlborough: His Life and Times* 4 vols (London: Sphere Books edn., 1967), I, p. 59.

3. Harris, *Passion for Government*, p. 17.

4. Ibid., p. 18.

5. Ibid., p. 19.

6. Ibid., p. 20.

7. Ibid., p. 21.

8. Ibid., p. 30.

9. Ibid., p. 37.

10. Churchill, *Marlborough*, I, p. 109.

11. *Private Correspondence of Sarah, Duchess of Marlborough* 2 vols. (London: Henry Colburn, 1838), I, p. 2.

12. Ibid., I, p. 128.

13. Ibid., I, p. 22.

14. Frances Harris, *The General in Winter: The Marlborough-Godolphin Friendship and the Reign of Queen Anne* (Oxford: Oxford University Press, 2017), p. 28.

15. Churchill, *Marlborough*, IV, p. 541.

16. Harris, *Passion for Government*, p. 61.

17. Ibid., p. 12.

18. Ibid., p, 1.

19. Ibid., p. 13, n. 34.

20. Ibid., p. 13.

21. Ibid., p. 1.

22. Ibid., p. 33.

23. Ibid., p. 36.

24. *Private Correspondence*, II, pp. 121, 123.

25. Churchill, *Marlborough*, I, p. 165.

26. Harris, *Passion for Government*, p. 34.

27. Ibid., p. 35.

28. Ibid., p. 54.

29. Ibid., p. 57.

30. Ibid., p. 40.

31. Ivor Burton, *The Captain-General: The Career of John Churchill, Duke of Marlborough, 1702-11* (London: Constable), p. 7.

32. Harris, *Passion for Government*, p. 63.

33. Ibid., p. 65.

34. Ibid.

35. Ibid., p. 66.

36. Ibid., p. 67.

37. Ibid., p. 78.

38. Ibid., p. 81.

39. Ibid., p. 89.

40. Harris, *General in Winter*, p. 107.

41. Harris, *Passion for Government*, p. 4.

42. Ibid., p. 5.

43. *Private Correspondence*, I, p. 12.

44. Ibid., I, p. 23.

45. Ibid., I, p. 29.
46. Ibid., I, p. 30.
47. Ibid., I, p. 24.
48. Ibid., I, p. 110.
49. Ibid., I, p. 36.
50. Churchill, *Marlborough*, III, p. 187.
51. Ibid., I, p. 40.
52. Churchill, *Marlborough*, II, p. 372.
53. Harris, *Passion for Government*, p. 113.
54. Ibid., p. 134.
55. Churchill, *Marlborough*, III, p. 266.
56. *Private Correspondence*, I, p. 115.
57. Burton, *Captain-General*, p. 165.
58. Churchill, *Marlborough*, III, p. 389.
59. *Private Correspondence*, I, p. 124.
60. Ibid., I, p. 201.
61. Ibid., I, p. 202.
62. Churchill, *Marlborough*, III, p. 392.
63. *Private Correspondence*, I, p. 212.
64. Ibid., I, p. 182.
65. Ibid., I, p. 227.
66. Ibid., I, pp. 232, 234.
67. Ibid., I, p. 248.
68. Churchill, *Marlborough*, IV, p. 190.
69. *Private Correspondence*, I, pp. 291, 295–9.
70. Ibid., I, pp. 339–44.
71. Ibid., I, p. 385.
72. Harris, *Passion for Government*, p. 5.
73. Ibid., p. 5.
74. *Private Correspondence*, I, pp. 367–8.
75. Harris, *Passion for Government*, p. 349.
76. Ibid., p. 1.
77. Ibid., p. 5.
78. Ibid., p. 4, n. 9.
79. Ibid., p. 3.

Chapter 2

1. Elizabeth Longford, *Wellington: The Years of the Sword* (London: Weidenfeld & Nicolson, 1969), p. 122.
2. Joan Wilson, *A Soldier's Wife: Wellington's Marriage* (London: Weidenfeld & Nicolson, 1987), p. 14.
3. Jane Wellesley, *Wellington: A Journey Through My Family* (London: Weidenfeld & Nicolson, 2008), p. 41.
4. Paul Cox, *Wellington: Triumphs, Politics and Passions* (London: National Portrait Gallery, 2015), p. 29.
5. Wilson, *Soldier's Wife*, p. 45.
6. Ibid., p. 47.
7. Wellesley, *Wellington*, p. 126.
8. Wilson, *Soldier's Wife*, p. 49.
9. Patrick Delaforce, *Wellington the Beau: The Life and Loves of the Duke of Wellington* (Barnsley: Pen & Sword, 2004), pp. 18–22.
10. Wilson, *Soldier's Wife*, p. 59.
11. Ibid.
12. Delaforce, *Wellington the Beau*, p. 29.
13. Wellesley, *Wellington*, p. 130.
14. Ibid., p. 131.
15. Wilson, *Soldier's Wife*, p. 72.
16. Delaforce, *Wellington the Beau*, p. 28.
17. Wilson, *Soldier's Wife*, p. 83.
18. Wellesley, *Wellington*, p. 176.
19. Delaforce, *Wellington the Beau*, p. 204.
20. Wilson, *Soldier's Wife*, p. 104.
21. Rory Muir, *Wellington: Waterloo and the Fortunes of Peace, 1814-52* (New Haven, CT: Yale University Press, 2015), p. 13.
22. Wellesley, *Wellington*, p. 179.
23. Wilson, *Soldier's Wife*, p. 119.
24. Ibid., p. 125.
25. Ibid., p. 128.
26. Wellesley, *Wellington*, p. 178.
27. Wilson, *Soldier's Wife*, pp. 122–3.
28. Ibid., p. 130.

29. Wellesley, *Wellington*, p. 183.
30. Wilson, *Soldier's Wife*, p. 135.
31. Wellesley, *Wellington*, p. 185.
32. Ibid., p. 192.
33. Wilson, *Soldier's Wife*, p. 152.
34. Wellesley, *Wellington*, p. 194.
35. Ibid., p. 4.
36. Muir, *Wellington*, p. 18.
37. Elizabeth Longford, *Wellington: Pillar of State* (London: Weidenfeld & Nicolson, 1972), p. 22.
38. Ibid., p. 22.
39. Delaforce, *Wellington the Beau*, p. 202.
40. Muir, *Wellington*, p. 18.
41. Ibid., p. 106.
42. Delaforce, *Wellington the Beau*, p. 203.
43. Muir, *Wellington*, p. 277.
44. Ibid., p. 263.
45. Longford, *Wellington: Pillar of State*, pp. 74–5.
46. Wellesley, *Wellington*, p. 202.
47. Longford, *Wellington: Pillar of State*, p. 75.
48. Ibid., pp. 75–6.
49. Longford, *Wellington: Pillar of State*, p. 76.
50. Ibid., pp. 76–7.
51. Ibid., p. 79.
52. Ibid., p. 74.
53. Delaforce, *Wellington the Beau*, p. 205.
54. Wellesley, *Wellington*, p. 205.
55. Francis Bamford and the Duke of Wellington (eds), *The Journal of Mrs. Arbuthnot* 2 vols (London: Macmillan & Co., 1950), II, pp. 35–6.
56. Wellesley, *Wellington*, p. 169.
57. Longford, *Wellington: Pillar of State*, pp. 34–5.
58. Ibid., pp. 180–1.
59. Delaforce, *Wellington the Beau*, p. 210.

60. Ian Fletcher (ed.), *For King and Country: The Letters and Diaries of John Mills, Coldstream Guards, 1811-14* (Staplehurst: Spellmount, 1995), p. 211.
61. Delaforce, *Wellington the Beau*, p. 65.
62. Muir, *Wellington*, p. 455.
63. Delaforce, *Wellington the Beau*, p. 153.
64. Muir, *Wellington*, pp. 293–4.
65. Ibid., p. 464.
66. Bamford and Wellington, *Journal of Mrs. Arbuthnot*, II, p. 220.
67. Delaforce, *Wellington the Beau*, p. 205.
68. Longford, *Wellington: Pillar of State*, p. 821.
69. Ibid., p. 198.
70. Bamford and Wellington, *Journal of Mrs. Arbuthnot*, I, pp. 422–3.
71. Ibid., II, pp. 5–6.
72. Delaforce, *Wellington the Beau*, p. 209.
73. Longford, *Wellington: Pillar of State*, p. 267.
74. Wellesley, *Wellington*, p. 245.
75. Longford, *Wellington: Pillar of State*, p. 267.
76. Wilson, *Soldier's Wife*, p. 162.
77. Wellesley, *Wellington*, p. 246.

Chapter 3

1. H.G. Moore Smith (ed.), *The Autobiography of Lieutenant General Sir Harry Smith* (London: John Murray, 1903, p. 69.
2. Ibid.
3. Ibid.
4. Ibid., p. 76.
5. A.L. Harington, *Sir Harry Smith: Bungling Hero* (Cape Town: Tafelberg Publishers, 1980), p. 7.
6. Moore Smith, *Autobiography*, p. 69.
7. Ibid., p. 70.
8. Ibid., p. 1.
9. Ibid., p. 74.

10. Harington, *Harry Smith*, p. 8.
11. Moore Smith, *Autobiography*, pp. 75–6.
12. Ibid., p. 74.
13. David Rooney and Michael Scott, *In Love and War: The Lives of General Sir Harry and Lady Smith* (Barnsley: Pen & Sword Military, 2008), p. 84.
14. Moore Smith, *Autobiography*, p. 144.
15. Ibid., p. 148.
16. Harington, *Harry Smith*, p. 42.
17. Joseph Lehmann, *Remember You Are an Englishman: A Biography of Sir Harry Smith* (London: Jonathan Cape, 1977), p. 146.
18. Ibid., p. 147.
19. Ibid., p. 186.
20. Ibid., p. 142.
21. Ibid., p. 148.
22. Ibid., p. 149.
23. Ibid., p. 155.
24. Ibid., p. 156.
25. Ibid., p. 183.
26. Ibid., p. 362.
27. Ibid., p. 183.
28. Ibid., p. 97.
29. Harington, *Harry Smith*, p. 38.
30. Ibid., p. 224.
31. Ibid.
32. Ibid.
33. Lehmann, *Remember*, p. 43.
34. Moore Smith, *Autobiography*, p. 133.
35. *Ladies of Waterloo: The Experiences of Three Women during the Campaign of 1815* (London: Leonaur, 2009), p. 262.
36. Moore Smith, *Autobiography*, p. 286.
37. Ibid.
38. *Ladies of Waterloo*, p. 263.
39. Moore Smith, *Autobiography*, pp. 183–4.

40. Lehmann, *Remember*, p. 56.

41. Ibid., p. 70.

42. Moore Smith, *Autobiography*, p. 213.

43. Ibid., p. 217.

44. Moore Smith, *Autobiography*, p. 218.

45. Rooney and Scott, *In Love and War*, p. 65.

46. Lehmann, *Remember*, p. 272.

47. Moore Smith, *Autobiography*, p. 7.

48. Ibid., pp. 82–3.

49. Lehmann, *Remember*, p. 36.

50. *The Smiths of Ladysmith* (Ladysmith Historical Society, 1972), p. 7.

51. Lehmann, *Remember*, p. 39.

52. Ibid.

53. *Smiths of Ladysmith*, p. 7.

54. Ibid., p. 8.

55. Moore Smith, *Autobiography*, p. 83.

56. *Smiths of Ladysmith*, p. 9.

57. Lehmann, *Remember*, p. 132.

58. Ibid., p. 133.

59. Ibid.

60. Ibid., p. 220.

61. Ibid., p. 223.

62. *Smiths of Ladysmith*, p. 18.

63. Lehmann, *Remember*, p. 224.

64. *Smiths of Ladysmith*, p. 19.

65. Lehmann, *Remember*, p. 224.

66. *Smiths of Ladysmith*, p. 5.

67. Lehmann, *Remember*, p. 36.

68. *Smiths of Ladysmith*, p. 5.

69. Moore Smith, *Autobiography*, p. 77.

70. *Smiths of Ladysmith*, p. 7.

71. Lehmann, *Remember*, p. 36.

72. Ibid., p. 118.

73. Ibid., p. 40.

74. Ibid., p. 118.

75. Moore Smith, *Autobiography*, p. 168.

76. Rooney and Scott, *In Love and War*, p. 107.

77. Harington, *Harry Smith*, p. 39.

78. Lehmann, *Remember*, p. 46.

79. Ibid., p. 46.

80. *Smiths of Ladysmith*, p. 21.

81. Ibid.

Chapter 4

1. Lady Sale, *A Journal of the Disasters in Affganistan, 1842* (London: John Murray, 1843), pp. 27–9.

2. Ibid., p. 10.

3. Shane Malhotra, '"If She Escapes She Will Publish Everything": Lady Sale and the Media Frenzy of the First Anglo-Afghan War, 1839-42', *Book History* 17 (2014), pp. 272–97.

4. Bawa Satinder Singh (ed.), *The Letters of the First Viscount Hardinge of Lahore to Lady Hardinge and Sir Walter and Lady James, 1844-47* Camden 4th ser. Vol. 32 (London: Royal Historical Society, 1986), p. 44.

5. Ibid., p. 46.

6. Noel St John Williams, *Judy O'Grady and the Colonel's Lady: The Army Wife and Camp Follower since 1660* (London: Brassey's, 1988), p. 99.

7. Malhotra, 'If She Escapes', p. 284, quoting *The Times*, 18 April 1843.

8. Sale, *Journal*, p. 38.

9. Ibid., p. 45.

10. Ibid., p. 48.

11. Ibid., p. 61.

12. Ibid., pp. ix–xvi.

13. Ibid., p. 64.

14. Ibid., p. 67.

15. Patrick Macrory, *Signal Catastrophe: The Story of the Disastrous Retreat from Kabul, 1842* (London: History Book Club, 1967), pp. 162–3, 168.
16. Sale, *Journal*, p. 82.
17. Ibid., p. 83.
18. Ibid., p. 86.
19. Ibid., pp. 98–9.
20. Ibid., p. 109.
21. Ibid., p. 116.
22. Ibid., p. 121.
23. Ibid., p. 120.
24. Ibid., p. 121.
25. Ibid., p. 131.
26. Macrory, *Signal Catastrophe*, p. 186.
27. Ibid., p. 201.
28. Sale, *Journal*, p. 124.
29. Ibid., p. 126.
30. Ibid., p. 133.
31. Ibid., p. 135.
32. Ibid., p. 187.
33. Ibid., p. 189.
34. Ibid., p. 192.
35. Ibid., p. 201.
36. Ibid., pp. 214–15.
37. Ibid., p. 219.
38. Macrory, *Signal Catastrophe*, p. 205.
39. Sale, *Journal*, p. 223.
40. Ibid., p. 227.
41. Macrory, *Signal Catastrophe*, p. 221, n. 1.
42. Verity McInnis, *Women of Empire: Nineteenth Century Army Officers' Wives in India and the US West* (Norman, OK: University of Oklahoma Press, 2017), p. 69.
43. Sale, *Journal*, p. 280.
44. Ibid., p. 281.

45. Ibid., p. 287.
46. Ibid., p. 288.
47. Ibid., p. 289.
48. Ibid., p. 298.
49. Ibid., p. 301.
50. Ibid., p. 319.
51. Ibid., p. 324.
52. Ibid., p. 331.
53. Ibid., p. 342.
54. Malhotra, 'If She Escapes', p. 276.
55. Ibid., p. 279.
56. Sale, *Journal*, pp. 399–400.
57. Ibid., p. 401.
58. Ibid., p. 404.
59. Ibid., p. 416.
60. Ibid., pp. 423–4.
61. Ibid., p. 426.
62. Ibid., p. 431.
63. Ibid., p. 433.
64. Ibid., p. 436.
65. Ibid., p. 438.
66. Malhotra, 'If She Escapes', pp. 285–7.
67. Macrory, *Signal Catastrophe*, p. 276.

Chapter 5

1. Elizabeth Butler, *An Autobiography* reprint edn. (Sevenoaks: Fisher Press, 1993), pp. 205, 208.
2. South Lanarkshire Council Museum, Wolseley Diaries, CAM.H.22, Diary, 11 Jun. 1877.
3. Lieutenant Colonel the Hon. H.D. Napier, *Field Marshal Lord Napier of Magdala* (London: Edward Arnold, 1927), p. 160.
4. Major General Sir Charles Callwell, *Stray Recollections* 2 vols (London: Edward Arnold, 1923), I, p. 218.

5. National Army Museum (hereafter NAM), Roberts Mss, 7101-23-100-3, Roberts to Cambridge, 15 Nov. 1890.

6. Royal Archives (hereafter RA), VIC/ADDE/1/12999, White to Cambridge, 1 Aug. 1893.

7. NAM, Roberts Mss, 7101-23-11, Brackenbury to Roberts, 6 Dec. 1892.

8. General Sir George Greaves, *Memoirs* (London: John Murray, 1924), pp. 168–9.

9. Hatfield House Muniments, Salisbury Mss, A/112/19, Cromer to Barrington, 3 Mar. 1899.

10. British Library (hereafter BL), Lansdowne Mss, L(5)21 Cromer to Lansdowne, 9 Nov. 1898.

11. BL, Lansdowne MSS, L(5)17, Cambridge to Lansdowne, 27 Jul. 1895.

12. Major General Sir Edward May, *Changes and Chances of a Soldier's Life* (London: Philip Allan & Co., 1925), pp. 141–2.

13. General Sir Charles Harington, *Plumer of Messines* (London: John Murray, 1935), p. 18.

14. Randolph Churchill, *Winston S. Churchill Companion Volume I Part II, 1896-1900* (London: Heinemann, 1967), p. 908.

15. Hove Public Library (hereafter HPL), Wolseley Mss, LW/P 5/4a, Lady Wolseley to Wolseley, 21 July 1879.

16. Christopher Brice, *The Thinking Man's Soldier: The Life and Career of General Sir Henry Brackenbury, 1837-1914* (Solihull: Helion & Co., 2012), pp. 68–74.

17. RA, VIC/ADDE/1/9685, Wood to Cambridge, 14 July 1881.

18. Mrs Walter Long, *Peace and War in the Transvaal: An Account of the Defence of Fort Mary* (London: Sampson Low & Co., 1882).

19. Ethel Grimwood, *My Three Years in Manipur and Escape from the Recent Mutiny* (London: Richard Bentley & Son, 1891).

20. Caroline Keen, *An Imperial Crisis in British India: The Manipur Uprising of 1891* (London: I. B. Tauris, 2015), pp. 163–7.

21. Cornwall County Record Office (hereafter CCRO), Pole-Carew Mss, CP/9, Nicholson to Pole-Carew, 30 Jun. 1891.

22. Queen Mary University Library, Lyttelton Mss, PP5/2/5, Lyttelton to wife, 8 Oct. 1891.

23. Charlotte, Lady MacGregor, *The Life and Opinions of Major General Sir Charles Metcalfe MacGregor* 2 vols (Edinburgh and London: William Blackwood & Sons, 1888), I, p. 320.

24. G.A. Leask, *Sir William Robertson* (London: Cassell & Co., 1917), pp. 45–6.

25. Craig Stockings, *Britannia's Shield: Lieutenant General Sir Edward Hutton and Late-Victorian Imperial Defence* (Port Melbourne: Cambridge University Press, 2015), pp. 64–5.

26. House of Commons Command Papers 1902 [C. 982], App. XV, p. 85.

27. BL, Carnarvon Mss, Add Mss 60800, Cunynghame to Carnarvon, 28 Nov. 1877.

28. M.W. Daly, *Empire on the Nile: The Anglo-Egyptian Sudan, 1898-1934* (Cambridge: Cambridge University Press, 1986), p. 41.

29. Warwickshire County Record Office (hereafter WCRO), Dormer Mss, CR895/92, Dormer to wife, 28 Oct. 1878.

30. WCRO, Dormer Mss, CR895/93, Dormer to wife, 23 Jun. and 28 Oct. 1884.

31. HHM, Salisbury Mss, A/53/68, Baring to Salisbury, 8 Dec. 1888.

32. Stephen Manning, *Evelyn Wood VC: Pillar of Empire* (Barnsley: Pen & Sword, 2007), pp. 57–61.

33. Stephen Manning, 'Evelyn Wood', in Steven J. Corvi and Ian F.W. Beckett (eds), *Victoria's Generals* (Barnsley: Pen & Sword, 2009), pp. 28–50, at p. 30.

34. HPL, Wolseley Mss, Wolseley Mss, LW/P 8/14/1, Lady Wolseley to Wolseley, 19 Oct. 1882.

35. HPL, Wolseley Mss, W/P, 13/22, Wolseley to Lady Wolseley, 1 Oct. 1884.

36. Campbell Collections, University of KwaZulu-Natal, Pietermaritzburg (hereafter KCL), Wood Mss, KCM 89/9/24/7, Colley to Wood, Jan. 1876.

37. RA, VIC/MAIN/O/16/24, Lady Wood to Queen, 14 Sep. 1882.

38. Sir George Arthur (ed.), *The Letters of Lord and Lady Wolseley, 1870-1911* (London: William Heinemann, 1922), p. 152.

39. HPL, Wolseley Mss, W/P 9/33, Wolseley to Lady Wolseley, 4 Oct. 1880.

40. HPL, Wolseley Mss, W/P 16/85, Wolseley to Lady Wolseley, 11 Oct. 1887.

41. HPL, Wolseley Mss, W/P 27/67, Wolseley to Lady Wolseley, 23 Aug. 1898.

42. RA, VIC/MAIN/W/10/82, Cambridge to Ponsonby, 19 Nov. 1888.

43. Liddell Hart Centre for Military Archives (hereafter LHCMA), Alison Mss, Box 2, Wood to Alison, 7 Dec. 1888.

44. KCL, Wood Mss, KCM 89/9/43/11, Herbert to Wood, 7 Dec. 1888.

45. RA, VIC/MAIN/O/35/117, Martin to Queen, Oct. 1879.

46. Alan James (ed.), *The Master, the Modern Major General and his Clever Wife: Henry James's Letters to Field Marshal Lord Wolseley and Lady Wolseley, 1878-1913* (Charlottesville, VA: University of Virginia Press, 2012), pp. xxvi–xxxii.

47. HPL, Wolseley Mss, W/P 8/24, Wolseley to Lady Wolseley, 11 Sep. 1879.

48. Kwa-Zulu Natal Archives, Wood Mss, II/2/11, Lady Wolseley to Lady Wood, 21 Jun. 1879.

49. General Sir Neville Lyttelton, *Eighty Years: Soldiering, Politics, Games* (London: Hodder & Stoughton, n. d. [1927]), p. 164.

50. HPL, Wolseley Mss, LW/P 10/18, Lady Wolseley to Wolseley, 16 Sep. 1884 and attached note by Frances Wolseley.

51. Adrian Preston (ed.), *Sir Garnet Wolseley's South African Journal, 1879-80* (Cape Town: A.A. Balkema, 1973), p. 322, n. 100.15.

52. HPL, Wolseley Mss, W/P 9/7, Wolseley to Lady Wolseley, 5–9 Feb. 1880.

53. HPL, Wolseley Mss, LW/P 4/4, Lady Wolseley to Wolseley, 16 Aug. 1878.

54. HPL, Wolseley Mss, W/P 8/4, Wolseley to Lady Wolseley, 4 Jun. 1879.

55. HPL, W/P 8/37, Wolseley to wife, 6–12 Dec. 1879.

56. John Pollock, *Kitchener: The Road to Omdurman* (London: Constable, 1998), p. 42.

57. HPL, Wolseley Mss, LW/P 11/15/6, Queen to Lady Wolseley, 5 Mar. 1885.

58. BL, Campbell Bannerman Mss, Add Mss 41233, Campbell-Bannerman to Lady Wolseley, 10 and 15 Nov. 1893.

59. RA, VIC/MAIN/W/15/124, Lady Wolseley to Bigge, 22 Dec. 1899.

60. James, *Master, Modern Major General and Clever Wife*, pp. 88–9.

61. 'Memorials to Lord Wolseley, Hampton Court', *The Architect and Builders' Journal*, 28 Nov. 1917.

62. HPL, Wolseley Mss, LW/P 11/7, Lady Wolseley to Wolseley, 11 Feb. 1885.

63. RA, VIC/MAIN/W/13/26, Ponsonby to Bigge, 16 May 1896.

64. NAM, Roberts Mss, 7101-23-52, Nicholson to Roberts, 2 Mar. 1897.

65. Marjory Pegram, *The Wolseley Heritage: The Story of Frances Viscountess Wolseley and Her Parents* (London: John Murray, 1939), p. 150.

66. BL, Asia, Pacific and Africa Collections (hereafter APAC), Burne Mss, Mss Eur. D951/8, Lytton to Burne, 7 Mar. 1878.

67. RA, VIC/MAIN/N/35/45, Lady Lytton to Queen, 7 Sep. 1878.

68. Sir William Butler, *The Life of Sir George Pomeroy-Colley* (London: John Murray, 1899), p. 279.

69. RA, VIC/MAIN/O/38/276, Wood to Queen, 27 Feb. 1881.

70. Joseph Lehmann, *The First Boer War* (London: Jonathan Cape, 1972), pp. 88, 234; Oliver Ransford, *The Battle of Majuba Hill: The First Boer War* (London: John Murray, 1967), pp. 71–2.

71. John Laband, *The Transvaal Rebellion: The First Boer War, 1880–81* (Harlow: Pearson Education, 2005), p. 189.

72. Duke University David M. Rubenstein Rare Book and Manuscript Library, Wolseley Mss, Wolseley to George Wolseley, 28 May 1891.

73. BL, Lansdowne Mss, L(5)48, Lansdowne to Roberts, 17 Aug. 1900.

74. BL, Lansdowne Mss, L(5)44, Bigge to Lansdowne, 18 Aug. 1900.

75. BL, Lansdowne Mss, L(5)44, Lansdowne to Bigge, 17 and 20 Aug. 1900; L(5)48, Roberts to Lansdowne, 18 Aug. 1900.

76. CCRO, Pole-Carew Mss, CP/128, Diary of a Staff Officer, 11 Apr. 1900.

77. HPL, Wolseley Mss, W/P 24/76 and 77, Wolseley to Lady Wolseley, both 1 Aug. 1895.

78. HPL, Wolseley Mss, W/W. 4/74, Wolseley to George Wolseley, 21 Jul. 1897.

79. HPL, Wolseley Mss, W/W.4/140, Wolseley to George Wolseley, 1 Nov. 1900.

80. CCRO, Pole-Carew Mss, CP/9, Nora Roberts to Pole-Carew, 5 Jan. 1883.

81. HPL, Wolseley Mss, LW/P 21/47, Lady Wolseley to Wolseley, 2 Jul. 1895.

82. RA, QM/PRIV/CC50/193, Prince Adolphus to his parents, 12 Nov. 1888; QM/PRIV/CC50/223, Prince Adolphus to Princess Augusta, Grand Duchess of Mecklenburg-Strelitz, 14 Feb. 1890.

83. NAM, Roberts Mss, 7101-23-104, Roberts to Cowell, 9 Aug. 1893.

84. RA, VIC/ADDU/32, Queen to Princess Royal, 26 Aug. 1895; BL, Lansdowne Mss, L(5)54, Salisbury to Lansdowne, 5 Aug. 1895.

85. APAC, Luard Mss, Mss Eur C.262, 7-8, Diary of Hugh Bixby Luard (written about 1937).

86. National War Museum of Scotland, Egerton Mss, M1994/112/92, 'Reminiscences of the 72nd Highlanders', 16 Feb. 1931, p. 4.

87. APAC, White Mss, Eur Mss F108/101(f), White to wife, 17 Jul. 1888.

88. Rodney Atwood, *The Life of Field Marshal Lord Roberts* (London: Bloomsbury, 2015), p. 152.

89. Rodney Atwood, '"So single minded a man and so noble-hearted a soldier": Field Marshal Earl Roberts of Kandahar, Waterford and Pretoria', in Ian F. W. Beckett (ed.), *Victorians at War: New Perspectives* (Society for Army Historical Research, Special Publication No 16, 2007), pp. 59–74, at p. 67.

90. Rodney Atwood, *Roberts and Kitchener in South Africa, 1900-02* (Barnsley: Pen & Sword, 2011), p. 295, n. 17.

91. General Sir Ian Hamilton, *Listening for the Drums* (London: Faber & Faber, 1944), p. 193.

92. Celia Lee, *A Soldier's Wife: Jean, Lady Hamilton, 1861-1947* (London: Privately published, 2001), p. 6.

93. LHCMA, Hamilton Mss, 1/2/9, Roberts to Hamilton, 27 Jul. 1893.

94. Thomas Pakenham, *The Boer War*, (London: Weidenfeld & Nicolson, 1979), pp. 448–9.

95. David James, *The Life of Lord Roberts* (London: Hollis & Carter, 1954), p. xiv.

96. National Library of Scotland, Minto Mss, MS 12378, Letters of Lady Roberts to Melgund.

97. National Library of Wales, Hills-Johnes Mss, L12996, Nairne to Hills-Johnes, 20 Mar. 1896.

Chapter 6

1. National Library of Scotland, Haig Mss, Acc. 3155/6c, Haig to sister, 17 Sep. 1902.

2. J. Paul Harris, *Douglas Haig and the First World War* (Cambridge: Cambridge University Press, 2008), p. 8.

3. The Countess Haig, *The Man I Knew* (Edinburgh: The Moray Press, 1936), p. 32.

4. Douglas Scott (ed.), *Douglas Haig: The Preparatory Prologue, 1861–1914 – Diaries and Letters* (Barnsley: Pen & Sword, 2006), pp. 6–7.

5. Haig, *Man I Knew*, p. 33.

6. Scott (ed.), *Douglas Haig*, p. 241.

7. Gary Sheffield and John Bourne (eds), *Douglas Haig: War Diaries and Letters, 1914-18* (London: Weidenfeld & Nicolson, 2005), p. 12.

8. Haig, *Man I Knew*, p. 44.

9. Ibid., p. 45.

10. Ibid., p. 46.

11. Ibid.

12. Ibid., p. 50.

13. Ibid., p. 55.

14. Ibid., p. 59.

15. Ibid., p. 56.

16. Ibid., p. 79.

17. Ibid., p. 80.

18. Ibid., p. 97.
19. Scott (ed.), *Douglas Haig*, pp. 301, 310.
20. Haig, *Man I Knew*, p. 103.
21. Ibid., p. 114.
22. Ibid., p. 115.
23. Ibid., p. 116.
24. Ibid., p. 117.
25. Ibid., p. 120.
26. Ian F.W. Beckett, 'King George V and His Generals', in Matthew Hughes and Matthew Seligmann (eds), *Leadership in Conflict, 1914-18* (Barnsley: Leo Cooper, 2000), pp. 247–64.
27. Sheffield and Bourne, *Haig: War Diaries and Letters*, p. 4.
28. Haig, *Man I Knew*, pp. 120–1.
29. Ibid., p. 124.
30. Ibid., p. 138.
31. Ibid., p. 165.
32. Harris, *Douglas Haig*, p. 108.
33. For the continuing debates on Haig as military commander, see Ian F.W. Beckett, Timothy Bowman and Mark Connelly, *The British Army and the First World War* (Cambridge: Cambridge University Press, 2017), especially pp. 277–344.
34. Haig, *Man I Knew*, p. 169.
35. Ibid., p. 180.
36. Ibid.
37. Harris, *Douglas Haig*, p. 50.
38. Haig, *Man I Knew*, p. 181.
39. Harris, *Douglas Haig*, p. 244.
40. Haig, *Man I Knew*, pp. 187–8.
41. Ibid., p. 199.
42. Ibid., p. 218.
43. Ibid., p. 219.
44. Ibid.
45. Harris, *Douglas Haig*, p. 428.

46. Ian F. W. Beckett, *Johnnie Gough VC: A Biography of Brigadier General Sir John Edmond Gough* (London: Tom Donovan Publishing, 1989), p. 206.

47. Eugene P. Ryan (ed.), *Haig's Medical Officer: The Papers of Colonel Eugene 'Micky' Ryan* (Barnsley: Pen & Sword, 2013), p. 87.

48. Gerard De Groot, 'The Reverend George S. Duncan at GHQ, 1916-18', in Alan J. Guy, R.N.W. Thomas and Gerard J. De Groot (eds), *Military Miscellany I* (Stroud: Sutton Publishing for Army Records Society, 1996), pp. 265–434, at p. 306.

49. Ryan, *Haig's Medical Officer*, p. 132.

50. Harris, *Douglas Haig*, pp. 446–7.

51. Ryan, *Haig's Medical Officer*, p. 195.

52. Ibid., p. 116.

53. Ibid., p. 166.

54. Ibid., p. 160.

55. Ibid., p. 158.

56. Ibid., p. 160.

57. Nigel Cave, 'Haig and Religion', in Brian Bond and Nigel Cave (eds), *Haig: A Reappraisal 70 Years On* (Barnsley: Leo Cooper, 1999), pp. 240–57; Gerard De Groot, *Douglas Haig, 1861-1928* (London: Unwin Hyman, 1988), p. 118.

58. De Groot, 'Duncan', p. 277.

59. Ibid., p. 294.

60. Ibid., p. 344.

61. Ibid., p. 404.

62. Beckett, Bowman and Connelly, *British Army*, pp. 345–88.

63. De Groot, 'Duncan', p. 405.

64. Haig, *Man I Knew*, p. 241.

65. Ibid., p. 284.

66. Harris, *Douglas Haig*, p. 519.

67. Niall Barr and Gary Sheffield, 'Douglas Haig, the Common Soldier and the British Legion', in Bond and Cave, *Haig: A Reappraisal*, pp. 223–39.

68. Haig, *Man I Knew*, p. 246.

69. Ibid., pp. 253–4.

70. Ibid., p. 254.

71. Ibid., p. 280.

72. Ibid., p. 292.

73, Ibid., p. 293.

74. Ibid., p. 295.

75. Ibid., p. 296.

76. Ibid., p. 297.

77. Ibid., pp. 297–8.

78. Ibid., p. 306.

79. Ibid., p. 310.

80. Ibid., p. 316.

81. Ibid., p. 318.

82. Ibid., p. 319.

83. Ibid., p. 272.

84. Keith Simpson, 'The Reputation of Sir Douglas Haig', in Brian Bond (ed.), *The First World War and British Military History* (Oxford: The Clarendon Press, 1991), pp. 141–62 at p. 143.

85. Haig, *Man I Knew*, p. 3.

86. Ibid., p. 203.

87. Ibid., p. viii.

88. Simpson, 'Reputation of Haig', pp. 150–1.

89. Barr and Sheffield, 'Haig, Common Soldier and British Legion', p. 225; Sergeant Thomas Secrett, *Twenty Five Years with Earl Haig* (London: Jarrolds, 1929).

Chapter 7

1. Alistair Horne with David Montgomery, *The Lonely Leader: Monty, 1944-45* (London: Macmillan, 1994), p. 17.

2. Ibid.

3. Nigel Hamilton, *Monty: The Making of a General* (London: Hamish Hamilton, 1981), p. 202.

4. Ibid., p. 204.

5.   Horne, *Lonely Leader*, p. 38.
6.   Hamilton, *Monty*, p. 207.
7.   Brian Montgomery, *A Field Marshal in the Family* (London: Constable, 1973), p. 203.
8.   Hamilton, *Monty*, p. 210.
9.   Field Marshal Viscount Montgomery, *Memoirs* (London: Collins, 1958), p. 42.
10. Horne, *Lonely Leader*, p. 6.
11. Hamilton, *Monty*, p. 229.
12. Ibid., pp. 246–7.
13. Ibid., p. 248.
14. Horne, *Lonely Leader*, p. 21.
15. Montgomery, *Memoirs*, p. 43.
16. Hamilton, *Monty*, p. 273.
17. Ibid., p. 274.
18. Ibid., p. 277.
19. Montgomery, *Memoirs*, p. 44,
20. Horne, *Lonely Leader*, p. 23.
21. Ibid., p. 24.
22. Montgomery, *Memoirs*, p. 44.
23. Horne, *Lonely Leader*, p. 39.
24. Ibid., p. xv.
25. Hamilton, *Monty*, p. 201.
26. Horne, *Lonely Leader*, p. 25.
27. Hamilton, *Monty*, p. 324.

Bibliography

Primary Sources

British Library, London: Campbell-Bannerman Mss, Carnarvon Mss, Lansdowne Mss.

British Library, Asia, Pacific and Africa Collections, London: Burne Mss, Luard Mss, White Mss.

Campbell Collections, University of KwaZulu-Natal, Pietermaritzburg: Wood Mss.

Cornwall County Record Office, Truro: Pole-Carew Mss.

Duke University David M. Rubenstein Rare Book and Manuscript Library, Durham, North Carolina: Wolseley Mss.

Hatfield House Muniments, Salisbury Mss.

Hove Public Library: Wolseley Mss.

Kwa-Zulu Natal Archives, Pietermaritzburg: Wood Mss.

Liddell Hart Centre for Military Archives, King's College, London: Alison Mss, Hamilton Mss.

National Army Museum, London: Roberts Mss.

National Library of Scotland, Edinburgh: Haig Mss, Minto Mss.

National Library of Wales: Hills-Johnes Mss.

National War Museum of Scotland, Edinburgh: Egerton Mss.

Queen Mary University Library, London: Lyttelton Mss.

Royal Archives, Windsor: Cambridge Mss, Main Series.

South Lanarkshire Council Museum, Hamilton: Wolseley Diaries.

Warwickshire County Record Office, Warwick: Dormer Mss.

Printed Primary Sources

Arthur, Sir George (ed.), *The Letters of Lord and Lady Wolseley, 1870-1911* (London: William Heinemann, 1922).

Bamford, Francis, and Wellington, Duke of (eds), *The Journal of Mrs. Arbuthnot* 2 vols. (London: Macmillan & Co., 1950).

Churchill, Randolph, *Winston S. Churchill Companion Volume I Part II, 1896-1900* (London: Heinemann, 1967).

De Groot, Gerard, 'The Reverend George S. Duncan at GHQ, 1916-18', in Alan J. Guy, R.N.W. Thomas and Gerard J. De Groot (eds), *Military Miscellany I* (Stroud: Sutton Publishing for Army Records Society, 1996), pp. 265–434.

Fletcher, Ian (ed.), *For King and Country: The Letters and Diaries of John Mills, Coldstream Guards, 1811-14* (Staplehurst: Spellmount, 1995).

James, Alan (ed.), *The Master, the Modern Major General and his Clever Wife: Henry James's Letters to Field Marshal Lord Wolseley and Lady Wolseley, 1878-1913* (Charlottesville, VA: University of Virginia Press, 2012).

Preston, Adrian (ed.), *Sir Garnet Wolseley's South African Journal 1879-80* (Cape Town: A. A. Balkema, 1973).

Private Correspondence of Sarah, Duchess of Marlborough 2 vols. (London: Henry Colburn, 1838).

Ryan, Eugene P. (ed.), *Haig's Medical Officer: The Papers of Colonel Eugene 'Micky' Ryan* (Barnsley: Pen & Sword, 2013).

Sale, Lady, *A Journal of the Disasters in Affganistan, 1842* (London: John Murray, 1843).

Scott, Douglas (ed.), *Douglas Haig: The Preparatory Prologue, 1861-1914 – Diaries and Letters* (Barnsley: Pen & Sword, 2006).

Sheffield, Gary, and Bourne, John (eds), *Douglas Haig: War Diaries and Letters, 1914-18* (London: Weidenfeld & Nicolson, 2005).

Singh, Bawa Satinder (ed.), *The Letters of the First Viscount Hardinge of Lahore to Lady Hardinge and Sir Walter and Lady James, 1844-47* Camden 4th ser. Vol. 32 (London: Royal Historical Society, 1986).

Memoirs and Biographies

Atwood, Rodney, *The Life of Field Marshal Lord Roberts* (London: Bloomsbury, 2015).

Beckett, Ian F. W., *Johnnie Gough VC: A Biography of Brigadier General Sir John Edmond Gough* (London: Tom Donovan Publishing, 1989).

Brice, Christopher, *The Thinking Man's Soldier: The Life and Career of General Sir Henry Brackenbury, 1837-1914* (Solihull: Helion & Co., 2012).

Burton, Ivor, *The Captain-General: The Career of John Churchill, Duke of Marlborough, 1702-11* (London: Constable, 1968).

Butler, Elizabeth, *An Autobiography* reprint edn. (Sevenoaks: Fisher Press, 1993).

Butler, Sir William, *The Life of Sir George Pomeroy-Colley* (London: John Murray, 1899).

Callwell, Major General Sir Charles, *Stray Recollections* 2 vols (London: Edward Arnold, 1923).

Churchill, Winston S., *Marlborough: His Life and Times* 4 vols (London: Sphere Books edn., 1967).

De Groot, Gerard, *Douglas Haig, 1861-1928* (London: Unwin Hyman, 1988).

Delaforce, Patrick, *Wellington the Beau: The Life and Loves of the Duke of Wellington* (Barnsley: Pen & Sword, 2004).

Greaves, General Sir George, *Memoirs* (London: John Murray, 1924).

Grimwood, Ethel, *My Three Years in Manipur and Escape from the Recent Mutiny* (London: Richard Bentley & Son, 1891).

Haig, The Countess, *The Man I Knew* (Edinburgh: The Moray Press, 1936).

Hamilton, General Sir Ian, *Listening for the Drums* (London: Faber & Faber, 1944).

Hamilton, Nigel, *Monty: The Making of a General* (London: Hamish Hamilton, 1981).

Harington, A.L., *Sir Harry Smith: Bungling Hero* (Cape Town: Tafelberg Publishers, 1980).

Harington, General Sir Charles, *Plumer of Messines* (London: John Murray, 1935).

Harris, Frances, *A Passion for Government: The Life of Sarah, Duchess of Marlborough* (Oxford: The Clarendon Press, 1991).

Horne, Alistair, with Montgomery, David, *The Lonely Leader: Monty, 1944-45* (London: Macmillan, 1994).

James, David, *The Life of Lord Roberts* (London: Hollis & Carter, 1954).

Ladies of Waterloo: The Experiences of Three Women during the Campaign of 1815 (London: Leonaur, 2009).

Leask, G.A., *Sir William Robertson* (London: Cassell & Co., 1917).

Lee, Celia, *Jean, Lady Hamilton, 1861-1941: A Soldier's Wife* (London: Privately printed, 2001).

Lehmann, Joseph, *Remember You Are an Englishman: A Biography of Sir Harry Smith* (London: Jonathan Cape, 1977).

Long, Mrs Walter, *Peace and War in the Transvaal: An Account of the Defence of Fort Mary* (London: Sampson Low & Co., 1882).

Longford, Elizabeth, *Wellington: The Years of the Sword* (London: Weidenfeld & Nicolson, 1969).

————————, *Wellington: Pillar of State* (London: Weidenfeld & Nicolson, 1972).

Lyttelton, General Sir Neville, *Eighty Years: Soldiering, Politics, Games* (London: Hodder & Stoughton, n. d. [1927]).

MacGregor, Charlotte, Lady, *The Life and Opinions of Major General Sir Charles Metcalfe MacGregor* 2 vols (Edinburgh and London: William Blackwood & Sons, 1888).

Manning, Stephen, *Evelyn Wood VC: Pillar of Empire* (Barnsley: Pen & Sword, 2007).

May, Major General Sir Edward, *Changes and Chances of a Soldier's Life* (London: Philip Allan & Co., 1925).

Montgomery, Brian, *A Field Marshal in the Family* (London: Constable, 1973).

Montgomery, Field Marshal Viscount, *Memoirs* (London: Collins, 1958).

Moore Smith, H.G. (ed.), *The Autobiography of Lieutenant General Sir Harry Smith* (London: John Murray, 1903).

Muir, Rory, *Wellington: Waterloo and the Fortunes of Peace, 1814–52* (New Haven, CT: Yale University Press, 2015).

Napier, Lieutenant Colonel the Hon. H.D., *Field Marshal Lord Napier of Magdala* (London: Edward Arnold, 1927).

Pegram, Marjory, *The Wolseley Heritage: The Story of Frances Viscountess Wolseley and Her Parents* (London: John Murray, 1939).

Pollock, John, *Kitchener: The Road to Omdurman* (London: Constable, 1998).

Roberts, Field Marshal Lord, *Forty-One Years in India* 30th [single vol.] edn. (London: Macmillan & Co., 1898).

Rooney, David, and Scott, Michael, *In Love and War: The Lives of General Sir Harry and Lady Smith* (Barnsley: Pen & Sword Military, 2008).

Secrett, Sergeant Thomas, *Twenty Five Years with Earl Haig* (London: Jarrolds, 1929).

The Smiths of Ladysmith (Ladysmith Historical Society, 1972).

Stockings, Craig, *Britannia's Shield: Lieutenant General Sir Edward Hutton and Late-Victorian Imperial Defence* (Port Melbourne: Cambridge University Press, 2015).

Wellesley, Jane, *Wellington: A Journey Through My Family* (London: Weidenfeld & Nicolson, 2008).

Wood, Field Marshal Sir Evelyn, *From Midshipman to Field Marshal* 2 vols (London: Methuen & Co., 1906).

Monographs

Atwood, Rodney, *Roberts and Kitchener in South Africa, 1900–02* (Barnsley: Pen & Sword, 2011).

Beckett, Ian F.W., Bowman, Timothy, and Connelly, Mark, *The British Army and the First World War* (Cambridge: Cambridge University Press, 2017).

Bleser, Carol K., and Gordon, Lesley J. (eds), *Intimate Strategies of the Civil War: Military Commanders and Their Wives* (New York: Oxford University Press, 2001).

Cox, Paul, *Wellington: Triumphs, Politics and Passions* (London: National Portrait Gallery, 2015).

Daly, M.W., *Empire on the Nile: The Anglo-Egyptian Sudan, 1898-1934* (Cambridge: Cambridge University Press, 1986).

Harris, Frances, *The General in Winter: The Marlborough-Godolphin Friendship and the Reign of Queen Anne* (Oxford: Oxford University Press, 2017).

Harris, J. Paul, *Douglas Haig and the First World War* (Cambridge: Cambridge University Press, 2008).

Hurl-Eamon, Jennine, *Marriage and the British Army in the Long Eighteenth Century: The Girl I Left Behind Me* (Oxford: Oxford University Press, 2014).

Keen, Caroline, *An Imperial Crisis in British India: The Manipur Uprising of 1891* (London: I. B. Tauris, 2015).

Laband, John, *The Transvaal Rebellion: The First Boer War, 1880-81* (Harlow: Pearson Education, 2005).

Lehmann, Joseph, *The First Boer War* (London: Jonathan Cape, 1972).

Macrory, Patrick, *Signal Catastrophe: The Story of the Disastrous Retreat from Kabul, 1842* (London: History Book Club, 1967).

McInnis, Verity, *Women of Empire: Nineteenth Century Army Officers' Wives in India and the US West* (Norman, OK: University of Oklahoma Press, 2017).

Pakenham, Thomas, *The Boer War* (London: Weidenfeld & Nicolson, 1979).

Prochaska, Frank, *Women and Philanthropy in Nineteenth Century England* (Oxford: Oxford University Press, 1980).

Ransford, Oliver, *The Battle of Majuba Hill: The First Boer War* (London: John Murray, 1967).

Trustram, Myna, *Women of the Regiment: Marriage and the Victorian Army* (Cambridge: Cambridge University Press, 1984).

Williams, Noel St John, *Judy O'Grady and the Colonel's Lady* (London: Brassey's, 1988).

Wilson, Joan, *A Soldier's Wife: Wellington's Marriage* (London: Weidenfeld & Nicolson, 1987).

Chapters and Articles

Atwood, Rodney, '"So single minded a man and so noble-hearted a soldier": Field Marshal Earl Roberts of Kandahar, Waterford and Pretoria', in Ian F.W. Beckett (ed.), *Victorians at War: New Perspectives* (Society for Army Historical Research, Special Publication No 16, 2007), pp. 59–74.

Barr, Niall, and Sheffield, Gary, in 'Douglas Haig, the Common Soldier and the British Legion', in Brian Bond and Nigel Cave (eds), *Haig: A Reappraisal 70 Years On* (Barnsley: Leo Cooper, 1999), pp. 223–39.

Beckett, Ian F.W., 'Women and 'Women and Patronage in the Late Victorian Army', *History* 85 (2000), pp. 463–80.

———————, 'King George V and His Generals', in Matthew Hughes and Matthew Seligmann (eds), *Leadership in Conflict, 1914-18* (Barnsley: Leo Cooper, 2000), pp. 247–64.

Cave, Nigel, 'Haig and Religion', in Brian Bond and Nigel Cave (eds), *Haig: A Reappraisal 70 Years On* (Barnsley: Leo Cooper, 1999), pp. 240–57.

Kirkwood, Deborah, 'The Suitable Wife: Preparation for Marriage in London and Rhodesia/Zimbabwe', in Hilary Callan and Shirley Ardener (eds), *The Incorporated Wife* (London: Routledge & Kegan Paul, 1984), pp. 106–19.

Malhotra, Shane, '"If She Escapes She Will Publish Everything": Lady Sale and the Media Frenzy of the First Anglo-Afghan War, 1839-42', *Book History* 17 (2014), pp. 272–97.

Manning, Stephen, 'Evelyn Wood', in Steven J. Corvi and Ian F.W. Beckett (eds), *Victoria's Generals* (Barnsley: Pen & Sword, 2009), pp. 28–50, at p. 30.

'Memorials to Lord Wolseley, Hampton Court', *The Architect and Builders' Journal*, 28 Nov. 1917.

Simpson, Keith, 'The Reputation of Sir Douglas Haig', in Brian Bond (ed.), *The First World War and British Military History* (Oxford: the Clarendon Press, 1991), pp. 141–62.

Index